FISH WHISTLE

BY DANIEL PINKWATER

Lizard Music

Alan Mendelsohn, The Boy From Mars

Yobgorgle, Mystery Monster of Lake Ontario

The Worms of Kukumlima

The Last Guru

Blue Moose

Return of the Moose

The Moosepire

Slaves of Spiegel

The Snarkout Boys and the Avocado of Death

The Snarkout Boys and the Baconburg Horror

The Muffin Fiend

Young Adults

Superpuppy (with Jill Pinkwater)

and others

FISH WHISTLE

COMMENTARIES, UNCOMMONTARIES
AND VULGAR EXCESSES

DANIEL PINKWATER

ADDISON-WESLEY PUBLISHING COMPANY, INC.
Reading, Massachusetts   Menlo Park, California
New York   Don Mills, Ontario   Wokingham, England
Amsterdam   Bonn   Sydney   Singapore   Tokyo
Madrid   San Juan

Many of the designations used by manufacturers and sellers to distinguish their products are claimed as trademarks. Where those designations appear in this book and Addison-Wesley was aware of a trademark claim, the designations have been printed in initial capital letters (e.g., Wonder Bread).

Most of these commentaries were broadcast on National Public Radio's "All Things Condsidered" between 1987 and 1989. Some of them appeared previously in other publications.

"Rhapsody in Glue" appeared in the June/July 1987 issue of *Air & Space/ Smithsonian*.

"Why I Don't Fly" appeared in the August/September 1988 issue of *Air & Space/Smithsonian*.

"Something There Is That Does Not Love a Mall" was published in the *Poughkeepsie Journal*.

"Talking to Kids" was produced on audio cassette in 1987 by The Children's Book Council.

Library of Congress Cataloging-in-Publication Data
Pinkwater, Daniel Manus, 1941–
    Fish whistle: commentaries, uncommentaries, and vulgar excesses/ Daniel Pinkwater.
       p.   cm.
    ISBN 0–201–51789–2
    I. Title.
    PS3566.I526F5   1989
    814'.54—dc 19   89–31127

Cover design by Janet Halverson
Text design by Patricia Dunbar
Set in 11-point Bodoni Book by Modern Graphics, Inc., Weymouth, MA

ABCDEFGHIJ-DO-89
First printing, July 1989

To Jill, who said, "For years I've had to listen to these stories at dinner parties, and now I find out you can boil them down to three or four minutes. Sheesh."

Acknowledgments

The author is grateful for the help advice and courtesy of Ira Glass, Art Silverman, the many friendly people who work on "All Things Considered," and Louise, whoever she may be, George Larson of Air and Space Magazine, in which Rhapsody in Glue and Why I Don't Fly first appeared, Jeanette Brodt and The Children's Book Council which issued Talking to Kids as a cassette, Lane Limited, makers of Edgeworth pipe tobacco, the management of La Parmigiana, exotic pizzerias of Kingston and Rhinebeck, New York, and the listeners who phoned and wrote to encourage, complain, elucidate, and forgive—without all of whom this book would have been impossible to make.

Contents

Introduction

Most of the pieces in this book, with a few exceptions (which are easy to spot because they're longer) were written as radio commentaries to be read on the National Public Radio news show "All Things Considered."

"All Things Considered" is a program to which I had listened for years. I had always admired it, but I became a really steady listener and fan when I came to live in the Hudson valley in New York State about nine years ago. Here I came to know the lovable indigenous folk, mostly as they've stood in my kitchen, scratching and breaking wind, and explaining that they wouldn't be able to fix the leaky gas line until the spring thaw, when their favorite wrench would doubtless turn up. It was then that I began to feel a need to be part of a community other than the one I live in.

"All Things Considered" went a long way toward providing that. It offers good news coverage, the features are interesting, and statements by anti-Semites are labelled as such.

I began to imagine that "All Things Considered" was, in a way, my home-town paper—a point of contact with a large number of people who tend to have three-digit I.Q.'s. It got so I depended on it. So it was exciting when I got a phone call that went like this:

"Mr. Pinkwater? Hi!"

"Hi."

"This is Louise."

"Hi, Louise."

"Would you like to do commentaries on the radio?"

"I've always thought I ought to."

"Neat! So you can be on 'All Things Considered,' OK? I'll tell Art you'll do it. 'Bye!"

"Wait!"

"Yes?"

"That's it? I just do commentaries? And who's Art?"

"Art Silverman. He's the producer. Thanks for saying yes. 'Bye!" End of conversation.

It so happened that, at the time, part of the irony that has characterized my so-to-speak professional life included my having been selected to give a recorded talk for the Children's Book Council, which is something like the Cheese Council, or the Hot Sausage Council—it's an outfit that promotes children's books. Annually they pick a few authors and illustrators and honor them by having them participate in the preparation of materials they send out during National Children's Book Week. Every year the promotion has a theme. This year the theme was something like "People Should Read Books."

(The reason my being a poster child was ironic was that the kiddie book industry had caught up with the greed decade and was in one of its periodic fits of hard-nosed commercial retrenchment. I wasn't earning a nickel. "We're not buying anything good this year," one editor told me.)

I eagerly accepted the assignment (there was an honorarium of $300 offered), and was sent to a local radio station to read my remarks. It was the first time I had been professionally recorded. When they played back the tape, I was impressed. I sounded good! I sounded a little like Jean Shepard, a hero of mine.

After my conversation with Louise, I reasoned that this Art Silverman, whoever he was, must have determined to put me on the program on the basis of my written work, which he had somehow seen somewhere. To make sure he didn't change his mind, I thought it might be a good idea to have a copy of the tape sent to him. So I called the nice woman at the Children's Book Council, and asked that a copy be sent to Art Silverman, at National Public Radio in Washington, D.C.

A week later, I got another phone call. This one was from Art Silverman.

"You want to do commentaries on 'All Things Considered'?"

"I thought I already was."

"Was what?"

"Doing commentaries on 'All Things Considered.' "

"How could you think that when I never heard of you before this morning? The people at the Children's Book Council sent me this tape, and I figured you'd be good on the program."

"But Louise called me last week and told me it was all set."

"Who's Louise?"

We never did work out what had happened, but I started doing commentaries for the program—and a great deal of fun it is. What's more, I can get published again! People involved with children's books rightly have contempt for anyone who wants to be connected with the industry—but a radio commentator! A radio commentator means . . . well, actually, nothing today, but the appelation still resonates from an earlier time. Now that I'm a commentator, I've been able to place some of the fiction they wouldn't touch before. I'm somebody! Very nearly.

So this is a story of how the medium of radio saved a Fat American from having to take a regular job. I find it inspiring.

FISH WHISTLE

CRACK THE WHIP
AND PASS THE CHIPS

Add Cold Water and Read

Ialmost had a job better than this. A real job. For the past
18 or 19 years I've been writing children's books. That's not
a real job—you can ask my mother.

Writing books for kids is a pleasure, but the business side
of it leaves a lot to be desired. So I was pretty excited when I
was approached by a public relations firm, representing a major
corporation. They wanted to give me a real job.

What they wanted was a spokesman. This public relations
firm wanted to know if I wanted to be a spokesman.

"It all depends. Spokesman for what?" I asked them. I wasn't
born yesterday.

It turned out that this major corporation was going to strike
a blow for literacy. They were going to put together a special
program which would persuade kids to read. Well—nothing
wrong with that.

I was supposed to go around and speak in behalf of books
and literacy, and this reading incentive program—and pudding.
Oh yes, this major corporation was introducing a new line of
pudding, and they hoped I would mention that too when I went
around talking about how good reading is.

The lady from the public relations firm said she hoped I would
have no objection to talking about pudding.

Well. I mean. Pudding. Pudding is pretty innocent. Pudding

never hurt anyone. I mean. Well. They were offering me a pretty decent salary. And, after all, reading *is* important. It's not as though they were promoting zip guns, or kiddie cigarettes— Pudding. Pudding is OK.

I said I'd do it. I figured out what I'd say:

Good evening ladies and gentlemen. Eat pudding. Books are good. Eat pudding. If kids read a lot. Eat pudding. They'll get so they can think clearly. Eat pudding. And if enough kids read and think. Eat pudding. We will have world peace. Eat pudding. Thank you very much. Eat pudding.

I figured I'd be a huge success.

The public relations people were going to check up on me and think it over. They said they'd let me know. Time passed.

Well, they called me. The lady from the public relations firm asked if I still wanted to do it.

"You bet," I said. "Eat pudding."

"Well the meeting with the major corporation is tomorrow," she said. "And we're going to tell them we want to go with you."

Picture this. The board room of the major corporation. The public relations people are there.

They say, "We've got this guy. He's written 50 books. The kids love him. Speaks real well. Loves pudding. And he wants to do it".

"Great," the people from the major corporation say.

"What's the guy look like?"

"We've got pictures right here."

Now, folks, I'm fat. Not just sort of fat. Not just pretty fat. I mean, *really* fat. I'm a fat guy. That's just how it is. Fat.

So the people from the major corporation look at the pictures and they start to scream, "MY GOD, HE'S FAT! THE MAN IS FAT! LOOK AT HIM—HE'S ENORMOUS! HE'S A TUB!"

The PR people realize they're dead. But they keep pitching. "Look at him, he's jumping around. He's very spry."

"THAT DOESN'T MAKE ANY DIFFERENCE! HE'S FAT!
WE CAN'T HAVE SOMEBODY SELLING PUDDING WHO'S
FAT! WHAT ARE YOU, CRAZY?"

Well, I didn't get the job. And here I am on Public Radio.
Eat Pudding.

Where Is the Grease of Yesteryear?

When I was fourteen, my family left Los Angeles, where we'd lived for five or six years, and moved back to Chicago. Naturally, I was glad to leave L.A., but I was miserable and lonely in Chicago.

I didn't know anybody. The high school I transferred to was a hotbed of early Elvis-worshippers and thugs. My parents rented an ugly apartment in a brand-new, shoddily built high-rise—a place I hated from the first day. And I was entering the state of adolescent crisis that lasted until I was thirty-two years old.

I spent my time wandering the streets. I liked walking through city streets, especially at night—and do so to this day. It was about this time that I began an earnest pursuit of the other activity which has characterized and shaped my life—gluttony.

My funds were limited, but I was able to sample many truly frightening varieties of 1950s junk food. When I hear experts inveigh against the fast food of today, which, if a little light in nutritional content, is at least fairly sanitary and made mostly of things you can eat, I remember such haunts of mine as Fred's Red Hots.

Fred's Red Hots was not far from the apartment building. It was in one of those triangular buildings you see where two streets converge diagonally. There were never a lot of customers at

6

Fred's. Just Fred. Angry face. Big nose. Grease-soaked apron. White paper cap. Mumbling.

Grease was the motif at Fred's. Instantly I would enter the place, a fine mist of grease suspended in the air would adhere to my eyeglasses—diffracting the light—so I always remember Fred's as a pointillist painting.

A monster fan over the door blasted grease-laden air out into the street, and made a roaring sound.

The red-hots I regarded more as objects of art than something to eat. Bright red, they tended to snap and squirt hot fat when you bit into them, and left a strange chemical taste in the mouth for days. Even I knew they were deadly, and left them alone.

I was a cheeseburger customer. Fred dispensed the cheapest cheeseburgers in Chicago. They came as singles, doubles, triples and quadruples. This referred to the number of patties of semiliquid fat and gristle. I believe a quadruple was under a dollar with a heap of dripping French fries, nearly raw in the middle, a limp quarter-pickle, and a bun with one last redundant gleam of schmaltz on top.

To make a balanced meal of a Fredburger, one could spoon on ketchup and scary bright-green pickle relish from bowls on the counter, thus adding vital trace minerals.

A quadruple contained more cholesterol than the average Copper Eskimo gets in a month. And indeed, most of my memories of Fred's are also of wild blizzards and eyeball-freezing February Chicago nights.

Not only did I thaw out at Fred's, and fortify myself for further wandering through the whiteout—Fred himself was, for the first few months I lived in Chicago, the only person I knew to speak to. I would tell Fred of my life, my suffering, my hopes and dreams.

"Yeh? So what?" Fred would ask, and give me a free limp, warm pickle spear.

It was good to know someone who listened.

Even after I began to make friends with various other misfits and delinquents, and have places to go and things to do, I would stop in at Fred's for a double or triple to fill the gap between the end of school and suppertime—or late at night, on my way home from committing an act of vandalism, I might drop by for one last infusion of lipids to help me sleep.

Probably the last time I visited Fred's was about the time I defied the predictions of guidance counselors and juvenile officers and left for college.

Seventeen or eighteen years later I was in Chicago with my wife. I drove Jill around the old neighborhood, and told her stories of my youth, which was at the very least misguided.

There was Fred's. Unchanged. I was charmed and filled with nostalgia.

"Let's go in," Jill said.

"Let's," I said. "But don't eat anything."

"Don't?"

"If you value your life."

We entered. I felt the grease-cloud envelop me. It was all exactly the same. Fred was exactly the same. It smelled exactly the same. The little greasy dust icicles hung from the transom exactly the same. Four or five Chicago cavemen sat at the counter, gnawing cheeseburgers.

"It's like stepping back in time," I whispered.

Jill, overcome with nostalgia on my behalf, ordered a red-hot.

"No!"

"It's fine," she said. "Just like the Bronx."

There is no arguing with Jill. She does as she pleases. Fred handed her the red-hot. Later she would pay the price of her arrogance.

"Do you recognize this man?" Jill asked Fred.

Fred eyed me.

"My husband used to come in here all the time, twenty years ago. He always talks about you. He says you were his only friend."

"Yeh? So what?" Fred replied.

It's not that you can't go home again. It's that most people know better.

Crack the Whip and Pass the Chips

I'd like people to start addressing me by my title. It's Captain. Captain Daniel Pinkwater. This is not a military appellation. When I was considered for service to my country, they weren't accepting any very fat soldiers. My captaincy has to do with my having been a professional dog trainer. Animal trainers are entitled to be called Captain.

Animal trainers are frequently of ample size. I don't know why this is. Working with dogs requires a good deal of activity, and it's hard on a fat man—but it's a fact—a good many of my fellow trainers, and some of the greats, are and have been fatsoes.

I never went deeply into the craft, and was only a full-fledged trainer for a couple of years before I drifted into the less honorable profession of writing. But in the time I worked in the field, and during years of apprenticeship and study, I was privileged to meet some legendary and very heavy masters of animal psychology.

As I write these words, Captain Bobby Gibbs may be on one of the highways of our land, at the wheel of an enormous truck, ingeniously laden with three elephants, five ponies, seven white

German shepherd dogs and a dromedary. I salute you, Captain Bobby. Not a month has gone by in the past ten years wherein I have not regretted my decision not to go with you, living the life of the road and learning to be an elephant trainer.

Captain Bobby was not the only over-300-pound practical animal behaviorist to see in me a likely disciple, able assistant, someone to eat tamales with, and perhaps the son he never had.

As a sprightly youth of 250 pounds or so, I caught the eye of many a senior trainer. They liked my style. Those listening in the South may have witnessed the truly artistic work of Uncle Heavy and his Porkchop Review. Popular at fairs and other events, Uncle Heavy with his troupe of pigs of every size has thrilled multitudes with displays of porcine prowess and intellect. Uncle Heavy picked me out of a crowd too—invited me to travel in the converted school bus with his pigs and his family ("Hell, boy—the pigs is *part* of the family"), learning the secrets of pig intelligence and working my way.

I turned him down too. What I took to be prior commitments and responsibilities caused me to hesitate, and, like Captain Bobby, he was gone—away in a cloud of diesel smoke. These men who can talk to animals are here today and gone tomorrow. The opportunity of learning how to get a porker to play the xylophone must be seized at the moment or lost.

How many of us, even once, are given the opportunity to live a life of pure glamour and adventure, good-fellowship and high-calorie meals? Here is one miserable storyteller who could at this moment have been putting a dromedary through its paces, astonishing the rubes with a breathtaking elephantine ballet.

I chickened out. I took the easy way. I chose to live out my life on paper instead of sending dogs through a flaming hoop.

I could have been like Captain Bobby—all belly and showmanship—cracking his whip after five fine horses, driving through the night to the next location, a bag of White Castle hamburgers by his side.

I don't know. The roads not taken. If he'd been asked, I'm pretty sure Hemingway would have gone.

A Wing and a Prayer

Several times I have tried to lose weight. It never worked out in the long run. My most notable effort was the time I went to a special fat clinic connected with a big university.

This place was run by a bunch of German doctors of just the right age.

They helped fat Americans to the tune of about three hundred dollars a week. The program consisted of being given two ounces of Rice Krispies twice a day and walking fifteen miles. It sure worked.

Of course, the patients tended to lose their motivation from time to time, and stop in at various eateries along their line of march. The fat patients were an important source of income in the town.

The patients were encouraged to believe that by means of esoteric tests, the medical staff were able to discover every unauthorized calorie in one's body—and even where it had come from. If you were a recidivist, and the doctors found out, they would take stronger measures. Hazel, a beautiful chick of about 400 pounds, told me this story:

Hazel was simply unable to stay with the Rice Krispies. She sinned continuously. So they locked her up in a hospital room on an absolute fast. Water only. The doctors explained to her,

13

"Ja, if you look like you are going to die, we will give you maybe a mashed banana."

Like most fat people, Hazel was intelligent and inventive. Right away, she corrupted the orderlies. She swapped rock and roll records for Hershey Bars and wrote checks for smuggled cheeseburgers.

Finally, she negotiated for a master key. This cost her the portable stereo and a lot of cash. The transaction was completed on a Wednesday in November. Late that night, she let herself out of her room, and wandered stealthily through the corridors of the hospital.

With that sixth sense all food hounds possess, she made her way to the basement, passed through a door, and found herself— in the kitchen. Alone. Not a soul in sight. The staff must have been on a break. And there on a table, piled high, were turkeys, dozens of them, just roasted. It was Thanksgiving eve.

Hazel made her move. Quick as thought, she selected a bird, tucked it under her nightgown, wrapped her robe around it, and split. The hot turkey burned against her skin, but like the Spartan boy with the fox, Hazel did not wince or cry aloud.

Safe in her room, Hazel made ready to gobble the gobbler.

Knocking off a whole turkey, let alone an industrial-size one, with no cranberry sauce or mashed turnips, is something not everyone can do—and Hazel was barely halfway through when she thought she'd had enough.

But what to do with the carcass? A half-devoured turkey lying around might arouse suspicion. Paranoia had set in. There would be a turkey count in the kitchen. A hospital-wide search. The German diet doctors would be called in. Her key would be discovered. Her parents, who were paying for all this, would be notified. Given Hazel's abilities, proclivities, and history, there seemed only one thing to do.

She did it. Every bit of it. She demolished the evidence. The bones she chewed to a pulp, and flushed. It was dawn by the time she had cleaned up every greasy trace of her crime.

Even a woman as capable as Hazel has her limitations. She was suffering from a great deal more than enough. As she sat in her room, in the early morning, she forswore turkeys. She cursed all turkeys. She hoped never to see a turkey again.

The lock clicked. It was one of the German doctors.

"Ja, Hazel, you have been such a good girl, we have brought you a surprise."

The surprise was two ounces of turkey—white meat without the skin.

Was this a trick? Had the purloined turkey been missed, and were they testing her? Hazel knew that to refuse protein in her situation would arouse suspicion.

She told me that getting that last two ounces down was harder than the last two pounds of the stolen bird. She told me that every dry, fibrous mouthful involved an eternity of mastication. She told me that to that very day, the smell of turkey had never quite left her nostrils. She told me this while we were waiting for our third pizza at Umbriaggo's House of Gravy.

Hazel survived her stay at the fat clinic, as I did. She came out of it relatively unmarked, except that she still makes sure to be somewhere out of North America in the month of November.

Fold on Line "B" and Ingest

Twice in the last couple of weeks, I have heard people not from New York City comment on the manner in which people who are from New York City address a slice of pizza.

They fold it. I'd never noticed this or given it much thought— but I lived in and around the big town for a number of years, and I'm a pizza folder myself.

This is what I mean by folding pizza. You are going to eat a slice of pizza. You grasp the slice firmly by the outer edge, where the crust is thick, and in one graceful movement, press a finger down in the center of the curve, and simultaneously gather the ends of the bisected arc together, causing a crease or trough to appear in the middle of the slice, extending from the edge toward the point. This has the effect of giving a measure of rigidity.

Holding the slice thus, keeping the fold intact, you convey the slice to the mouth, and begin to ingest it, like all civilized people, by nibbling the pointy part.

The outlanders want to know why New Yorkers eat pizza this way. I hadn't been aware that everybody didn't.

"How do you eat it?" I asked.

They eat it two-handed, supporting the tip of the slice with a finger, or pick up the thing, waving like a flag, and dive at it, turning the head sideways and snapping with the teeth. In some places I've been in the Midwest, the problem is more or less solved by chopping pizza into little squares, and by creating a thick crust like Wonder Bread. But I will not disgust the listener by dwelling on such practices, nor those who use a knife and fork or pluck at the thing, tearing off messy morsels.

Now that I'm discussing it, I do remember, in my unenlightened youth, struggling with unfolded pizza—but once I was exposed to the one true way, I never looked back.

Obviously, if you are going to deal with a slice in the public street, retire from the little window as soon as you've been served—so the next customer can step up, and manage a paper cup full of papaya juice and keep a folded newspaper under your arm—the slice has to be kept somewhat rigid. There is also the question of dripping grease and where it is apt to drip.

Born New Yorkers can handle the pizza and the papaya juice and READ the newspaper . . . while running for a bus.

These are just some preliminary thoughts on the subject. I present them as a public service. I'd be interested in developing a comprehensive study, if a grant is available.

Psychopathia Snacksualis

[This was an assignment from "All Things Considered" to go with a piece about phone sex. I got an actress named Scarlett O'Gronsky to play Tanya, and she did such a good job that the producers refused to run the piece. Too dirty.]

TANYA: This is Tanya, your love slave.

DMP: Uh, is this the number where you . . . uh.

TANYA: You get your fantasy fulfilled, honey.

DMP: It can be anything?

TANYA: Anything, honey. I'm all yours.

DMP: Well, I mean, this might be a little . . . strange.

TANYA: I'll talk about anything you want, you big strong hand-some man.

DMP: Nobody has to know about this, right?

TANYA: It's just between you and me, lover.

DMP: OK, I want to do it.

TANYA: Oooh, I can hardly wait, sweet man.

DMP: OK. . . . Tanya, it's a shore dinner.

TANYA: I don't think I know that one.

DMP: You know, a clambake. Steamed lobster, clams, beer.

TANYA: Yes?

18

DMP: Maybe mussels. Some crabs. Corn on the cob. Lots of
        drawn butter.

TANYA: What do we do with all that?

DMP: We eat it. I like some lemon in the melted butter.

TANYA: We just eat it?

DMP: You pretend like you're serving it to me. Start with a
        lobster.

TANYA: I'll try. I've got this . . . big . . . red . . . gorgeous
        . . . lobster for you, lover.

DMP: Yeh. Give me a claw.

TANYA: I'm twisting off a claw. Ooo! It's so big!

DMP: Dig out the meat. Dig out the meat.

TANYA: I'm dipping it in butter. Mmmm, hot, melty butter.

DMP: Oh, yes! Gimme!

TANYA: Putting the lobster in your little mouthie.

DMP: More! More!

TANYA: Don't be greedy, sweetheart. You want some clams?

DMP: Clams! Give me clams!

TANYA: Oooh! I'm geting so hot. I want some ice-cold beer!

DMP: Me too! I want beer!

TANYA: Oh. I'm popping the top. So frosty. Oh.

DMP: Yeh! Yeh! This is great. Now the corn on the cob.

TANYA: With salt and pepper, lover?

DMP: And butter! Lots of butter!

TANYA: Having fun?

DMP: This is wonderful!

TANYA: Look, you seem to be a really nice guy, but I'm going
        to have to hang up now.

DMP: No! We were going great!

TANYA: I know, but it's my lunch break. I'm going to call out for a pizza.

DMP: Just a little more. Let's talk about baked potatoes.

TANYA: No, really, sweetie, I'm starving. You want to talk to one of the other girls?

DMP: Naw. I guess not. Thanks, Tanya.

[*Hangs up.*]

Wow, after all that talking, she eats pizza on her own time. She must be some woman.

Something There Is That
Does Not Love a Mall

I had a good time in a shopping mall. I can't remember that ever happening before. Not that I don't use malls. I'm an American just like you, and I go to the mall to see movies, buy vitamins, and get healthy exercise walking up and down. It's just that I've never enjoyed the experience as such.

This took place in a brand-new mall—the first really fancy one in this area. I went there on opening day. I had no intention of going—I was just driving around and sort of happened upon it.

It's one of those two-story jobs, and the roof is translucent. Marble floors, columns and staircases, ficus trees. It's not exactly a high order of architecture, but the spaces and the light were really sort of pleasant. It reminded me of those gallerias they have in Europe.

And they were playing classical music on the sound system. Vivaldi flute sonatas. It was a good sound system. I felt better and better as I strolled around.

There's a section of food concessions, and white enamel tables and chairs. I got myself an iced coffee and sat in the food court, listening to chamber music.

"This is too good to keep to myself," I thought. I went home and got my wife. "I'm taking you out to lunch," I said.

"McDonald's or Burger King?" she asked me.

"Wait and see."

We drove to the mall. It was even better than my first visit. They were playing Mozart now. The people were having an awfully good time. They were walking around, smiling, sitting and eating, speaking quietly. They cleaned up their tables after they finished. They looked relaxed and happy. We felt relaxed and happy.

There was a Greek food booth. We love Greek food. Jill had spanakopita. I had moussaka. Not bad. Not bad at all.

"This is fantastic," Jill said. "I feel all energized."

"I wonder where all these civilized-looking people came from," I said. Many of the folks who live around here drive those pickups with the extra-big wheels and keep pit bulls.

"You're right," Jill said. "They all look strangely human."

We woke up lusting for stuffed grape leaves the next morning.

"Lunch at the mall?" I asked Jill.

"Let's go."

We arrived at the mall, and hurried in. Happy. But not for long. Today they were not playing classical music on the sound system. Instead it was middle-of-the-road, fusion, plastic elevator disco jazz. With plenty of percussion.

The patrons looked bugged. They were shouting to be heard over the music. Kids were crying. Mothers were belting kids. Men and women were hollering at each other. In the food court, people were tossing their garbage around.

The girl in the Greek food booth got our order wrong and I snarled at her.

As we bolted our food, I noticed what a cheap look the place had. Those preposterous columns and tacky, ostentatious mirrored ceilings. A little kid at the next table threw up his pizza, and his mother whacked him on the head.

It turns out the classical music was just turned on for the opening day celebration. Today it was business as usual.

There's supposed to be a marketing psychology theory that people who are agitated, angry and uncomfortable are more likely to make rash purchases. Remember those stories about how flickering lights in supermarkets encourage people to buy more microwave waffles?

Leaving the mall, in the parking lot, we nearly got run over by a bright blue pickup truck with four-foot-high wheels.

Who Only Stand and Snarl

This is addressed to all those people who work in the honorable profession of serving food to the public. Waiters, waitresses, kids behind the counter—if somebody, particularly me, wants to give you back a utensil, or vessel—don't give them a hard time—just give them another one.

I don't know if this is something that just happens in my neighborhood, or if it happens all over the country. I go into a restaurant, and there's something floating in my glass of water, or I've got a dirty fork.

So I say to the waiter or waitress, "May I have another fork?"

And they study it.

They hold it up to the light. They turn it around and around. Sometimes they ask, "What's the matter with it?"

"It's got a curse on it. It has dried wildebeest guts on it. Just bring me another one."

They go away, shaking their heads.

Sometimes they congregate with other waiters or waitresses in the back of the restaurant, and talk it over, gesturing at me.

About one time in three, when I reject a utensil, the server responds, "I don't see anything wrong with it."

This implies that I'm a paranoid personality. Next I'm going to complain that there are hedgehogs milling around under the table.

24

"Look, I don't want to discuss it. I don't like this fork. Just bring me another one."

More head shaking. My God, we could run this restaurant flawlessly if it weren't for those blasted customers. Back to the waitresses' station. "He wants another fork. Can you beat it?"

Today I was in a fast-food restaurant. One that has a salad bar. When you opt for the salad bar, the kid behind the counter gives you a plastic foam plate. Mine had a smudge of what looked like cigarette ash on it.

"Let me have another one of these, please," I said to the high-school girl.

She held the plastic foam plate up as though she were reading from it.

"Look," I said. "I'll tell you a secret about being a waitress. When a customer hands something back to you like that, don't examine it. Just take his word for it that there's something wrong with it, and gracefully hand him a new one."

"Why don't you keep your opinions to yourself?" the high-school girl said.

She was right, of course.

Nobody likes a complainer.

And a little dirt never hurt anybody.

IF MILK DUDS BE THE
FOOD OF LOVE

A Hot Time in Nairobi

Years ago, I stayed in a hotel in Nairobi. It was called Brunner's. I think it had been called the Queen Victoria, or something like that, before independence. Most tourists used to stay in the famous Norfolk Hotel, or the Hilton. Brunner's Hotel was a utilitarian, old-fashioned place in the business district. Made of stucco, bath down the hall, concrete floors, painted dark red. Every afternoon, a guy would come in with a Flit gun and spray under the bed. No frills. I liked it.

Downstairs there was a lounge where you could see and get into conversations with all kinds of people—petty government officials, professional hunters, guys who sold—I don't know—farm implements, and experienced shoestring tourists from all over the world.

One time I spotted a guy with long white whiskers, a beat-up tropical suit and horn-rims mended with tape. He looked like some huge wading bird—a relic of the empire—a classic English eccentric. I knew if I could get him talking, he would have plenty to say. He was sucking cigarettes right down to his teeth. I offered him a Lucky Strike. That was all it took. He was just waiting for someone to tell stories to.

It turned out the old guy was an itinerant teacher. He'd left England fifty years before, and had never gone back—teaching in every remote and exotic place on earth. He had something

29

to say about everything, and a wonderful way of saying it. All I had to do was keep feeding him American cigarettes. I was having a good time.

He told me he was currently headmaster of a school in some far-off part of Kenya. His assignment before that was in Peru— and he had with him a Peruvian kid he'd adopted—literally picked him out of a gutter as an infant. Now the kid was nine or ten, and was staying with him at Brunner's Hotel along with one of his school friends.

The two boys had been out wandering around Nairobi, and the old teacher was waiting for them to arrive. He invited me to join them all for supper.

The boys showed up. Two bright kids, well-spoken and knowledgeable. There wasn't any question that the old educator ran a first-class school.

At Brunner's you could eat in the dining room, or get a meal in the bar. The Europeans tended to gravitate to the dining room. The bar was altogether more cozy. You were likely to encounter local residents, dropping in for a snort, a snack and some conversation. Naturally, we ate in the bar.

I was feeling pretty good. This was just the sort of thing I'd come to Africa for. The old guy was a hundred percent authentic. For all I knew, at the end of the meal he was going to spread out a yellowed old map and propose we all go off in search of King Solomon's mines. If he did, I was ready to go.

The Thursday special was chicken curry. We all ordered it. They did it right. The waiter brought us a bunch of little plates of condiments, toasted coconut, chutneys, dhal, peanuts, flakes of fish trouve, and some played-out-looking little pale-green sections of chili pepper.

One of the kids said, "Mr. Pinkwater, you probably aren't used to eating curry. You want to be careful of those chilies."

"Kid, you obviously have no inkling who you're eating with," I told him. And I went on to fascinate the two boys with stories of death-defying pepper-eating among the Poles of Chicago, of whole towns wiped out by a single pepper in the southwestern United States, the dreaded Arizona firecracker, and the jalapeños that are individually shipped, packed in cotton and labeled "High Explosives."

"It's entirely a question of mind over matter," I explained to the boys. "You simply ignore the pain, and enjoy the flavor. You'll understand things like this better when you're grown up."

While I was educating them, I was spooning various good things onto my curry—including the chilies. They were clearly a mild and inferior variety. I wished we'd been served something formidable, so I could really show off.

Two mouthfuls later, I was in the throes of the most complete agony I have ever known. I have been disappointed in love. I have endured gall-bladder disease, said to produce the worst pain known to man. I have had my great toe crushed by a huge stone. These were nothing compared to the effect of those damned peppers.

I wept copiously. I sweated. I gulped water. For a time, my heartbeat and respiration were suspended, and my disembodied spirit hovered above the table, observing the old Englishman and the two kids, chewing complacently and watching my death agony. For a moment, I believe I began the journey through the long tunnel, and was dimly aware of Diamond Jim Brady, Fatty Arbuckle, Oliver Hardy and Orson Welles, waiting to welcome me on the other side.

Then, I was drawn back into my body. I sat sobbing and gasping at the little table.

"See? I told you to be careful of the chilies," the kid said.

It's a lesson I've never forgotten. It doesn't matter who you are, or what you've done, or think you can do. There's a confrontation with destiny waiting for you. Somewhere, there is a chili you cannot eat.

The Schmo of Kilimanjaro

My friend Ken Kelman is a genius—a playwright and film critic. He's lived his whole life in Manhattan, and, I believe, until he was a grown adult, never had an unobstructed view of the sky. Certainly, outside of the zoo—and the occasional dog, cat and rat in the street—he'd never seen anything of the natural world. What he did, mainly, was sit in dark theaters.

For some reason—I still don't know why—he agreed to take a trip to Africa with me.

I explained to Kelman that something we'd be doing a lot of on our trip would be going around in a wilderness, spotting animals.

"That's OK by me," Kelman said. He was ready to have a good time.

Given that Kelman had never been out of doors except to go from one building in Manhattan to another, I thought I might give him a sort of crash course in wildlife watching.

A good thing about New York City is the proximity of large state parks and rural areas. If you don't live there, this might never occur to you. Within an hour or two of midtown, I have seen eagles, foxes, flights of geese, beaver dams, and have walked miles of forest trails.

I decided to take Kelman along a stretch of the Appalachian

Trail, and point a few things out to him. He liked the idea. We drove about an hour and a half up the Taconic Parkway, and started walking. It was a good day for fauna. It was like a Disney nature film. Every few yards there was some woodland creature or other.

Kelman missed them all.

"Look! A red-tailed hawk!"

"Where? Where?"

The hawk waited as long as it could—but Kelman never focused on it.

"Shh! Look! Deer!"

"Deer? Where!"

I decided to concentrate on one species. Chipmunks. There were chipmunks by the thousand, romping around in the underbrush. As we walked, I tried to point one out to my friend. Never did he lay eyes on one. At times it was hard to progress without squashing one—but did he see one? He did not.

I was exasperated.

On the way back to the car, there, sitting on a stump, was a chipmunk—a fat, insolent one.

It didn't move.

Kelman noticed it.

He stared at it.

It stared at him.

"That a chipmunk?" Kelman asked.

"That is a chipmunk."

He looked some more. "Close to a cat," he said.

So we flew to Africa. He wasn't on the ground for two hours before a large animal had its claws on him. We'd dropped off our bags at Brunner's Hotel, and gone straight out to the animal orphanage at the Nairobi Game Park. This is a sort of zoo where foundlings and wild pets that have grown up are kept. The management encourages many of the inmates to go over the wall, and live free in the game preserve.

There were a bunch of bears, confiscated from an Indian circus for abuse. Kelman leaned up against the stock-wire enclosure to take a picture, and one of the bears grabbed him by the jacket.

"Hey! Cut it out!" Kelman giggled.

I dragged Kelman away from the bear. The bear had a good hold on him.

"Quit horsing around!" Kelman said to me. "I'm trying to take a picture."

"That bear was trying to drag you through the fence!" I said.

"Sure. That's what I would do if I were a bear," Kelman said.

Later, when we were actually on safari, he told me one morning that he wanted to find someone to complain to. He was mad. It seems a big yellow dog had been running around outside the tent, making noise in the night. It woke Kelman up and he finally had gone out and chased it away.

"People should tie up their dogs at night."

I went out, and sure enough, there were some good footprints, about nine inches across.

"Kelman, that was no dog. That was a lion."

"Well, what was it acting like a dog for? I hate it when I don't get a good night's sleep."

The Africans are still telling stories about Ken Kelman.

Direct from a Triumphant
Engagement in Karachi

When Ken Kelman and I were traveling in Africa, we hired a professional driver for our rented Volkswagen bus— Hassan Gull.

Hassan was a Pakistani, born in Kenya, and he was the best safari driver in the business. He told us so himself. He looked like Ronald Colman, pencil moustache, crisp green safari suit, hat with leopard-skin band. He was sharp. He made us look like a couple of bums.

"Bosses, you are going to have a wonderful trip," Hassan said. "I have never killed a tourist yet!"

However, he had come close. On that first morning, he chatted away, cataloging all the wrecks and close calls he—and whoever had been with him—had experienced. He wasn't just bragging either. We had one crash in a remote wilderness, an incident— entirely his fault—with a spitting cobra, some minor injuries, and several evenings spent with various characters wanted by the law—friends of his.

Naturally, we loved him. Our only complaint was that he had more fun than we did. It turned into his safari, with us as spectators or baggage. It got so that if something dangerous wanted doing, Kelman and I would knock each other down in our haste to be the one exposed, and thus deprive Hassan of the story.

36

What I want to tell you about was Hassan's joke. Every night, we would come to our scheduled resting place, usually a permanent tent camp. We'd have our supper, and then retire to the lounge tent or campfire. The tourists and drivers would gather, and Hassan would tell his joke.

This is the joke, as Hassan told it:

"Ladies and gentlemen, get a load of this. There was a man, and he wanted to catch a train. So he said to his wife, 'Pack me a lunch!' And he went to the railway station, and he waited for his train, and he went to sleep, and he missed his train."

Here Hassan would pause, his eyes sparkling—and then the punch line:

"He was daft!"

That was the joke.

When he told it the first night of the trip, we coughed and tittered politely. After all, Hassan was our employee and guide. We had to show some loyalty.

The next day, Kelman whispered to me, "Do you think he's going to tell the joke again tonight?"

"What's to stop him?"

He told it, of course. In a new camp, there was a new audience. We forced laughter, a little more hearty. I noticed the utter confusion in the eyes of the others—many of whom were British, and thus never sure if they'd gotten a joke or not. A few of them laughed a bit, out of politeness.

The next night, in front of a blazing fire in the Serengeti—

"Ladies and gentlemen, get a load of this. There was a man, and he wanted to catch a train. So he said to his wife, 'Pack me a lunch!' And he went to the railway station, and he waited for his train, and he went to sleep, and he missed his train. . . . He was daft!"

I exploded, when he got to the punchline. So did Kelman.

We were looking at the dismay and confusion on the faces of the other tourists. And Hassan's expression of triumph.

The next night, on the rim of the Ngorongoro Crater: "There was a man, and he wanted to catch a train."

Kelman and I were already guffawing and snorting.

"They're heard this before. So he wanted to catch a train. . ." I was seeing everything through a film of tears, pounding on a table, moaning with mirth.

"He was daft!"

Kelman and I were roaring and screaming. So were about half the other tourists.

The next morning, Hassan said, "That really is some good joke, isn't it, bosses?"

"Hassan, that is the funniest joke ever told."

"It's not just the joke, bosses. You have to know how to tell it."

Sharper Than a Steel-belted Radial

Earlier this summer, I killed a copperhead in my kitchen. I'd lived through this very scene so many times in nightmares that the real event, having the quality of a dream, didn't bother me a bit.

To those nature lovers who will be moved to send me letters of instruction, it is my policy, in the case of venomous reptiles in the house or on my doorstep, to dispatch them without remorse. I am not open to argument about this.

I'm not phobic about snakes, just the next thing to it. My friend Ken Kelman is afraid of pictures of snakes. Keeping to the sidewalks of Manhattan, as he usually does, he doesn't have to give the real thing a thought.

When Kelman and I took a trip to Africa, we had a run-in with a serious snake—a spitting cobra. This is a variety that can spit in your eye and blind you, from ten feet away, and then bite you for good measure. Hassan, our cheerful driver, spotted it in the road.

"Bosses, you want me to run him over and make him mad?"

"Hassan, we're surprised at you. You should know better than to molest animals."

"It's just a snake. If I run him over, he'll get excited, and you can take a swell picture."

While we were having this conversation, the snake was making up his mind what to do about us. He did a number of things directly contrary to all the snake books I'd ever read. One thing I'd always read is that snakes are shy and retiring, and will never attack unless cornered. This snake had all of Africa into which he could have escaped. Instead, he went for us.

We were in an old Volkswagen bus, hanging out the window, looking at him, quite high off the ground. The other thing he did, which the snake books say snakes can't, was leave the ground. According to the text, snakes aren't supposed to be able to strike more than one-third the length of their bodies—something like that. Well, I am able to tell you, some snakes can jump—if they see something they really want—like Kelman.

It was Kelman he was after; I'm pretty sure of that. Animals lunge at him. He brings something out in them. Hatred, probably, or love.

Kelman is usually tentative and hesitant in his movements. When the spitting cobra sprang, Kelman moved with amazing swiftness. He shut all the windows of the van, closed the open sunroof, pressed all the locks and buttoned up his coat, all while the thing was at the apogee, looking in at the window with an unpleasant smile on its face.

Then the snake slithered under the bus. We didn't see it appear on the other side.

"See? You should have let me run it over," Hassan said.

We drove on. After a few minutes, we had a flat tire.

"Hassan, get out and change the tire."

"Why me?"

"Because it's your job. You expect us tourists to change the tire?"

"You expect me to risk my life? That cobra bit the tire. Now it's wrapped around the axle, waiting to get me."

"Come on, Hassan. Snakes don't bite tires and wrap themselves around axles."

"Oh, now you know all about what snakes do! Weren't you just telling me no snake can jump up off the ground?"

In the end, all three of us dismounted, and changed the tire together, putting our hands on it in unison. It was a brand-new tire, and there were two little punctures in the sidewall. We didn't see the cobra—but I thought I heard raspy laughter coming from the tall grass at the side of the road.

In the Land of the Rising Pickle

In 1967 I traveled nonstop from Nairobi to Tokyo in search of delicatessen. Jewish deli. If they didn't have it in Japan, I was going to go straight on to San Francisco. I made stops in Aden, Bombay, Bangkok and Hong Kong. The trip took 27 hours. I flew in three different airplanes and read four novels on the way. I refrained from eating much airplane food. I wanted to keep my palate clear for pastrami.

My brother, Marlowe, who lived in Tokyo, met me at the airport. It was one in the morning.

"You look terrible," my brother said.

"Gimme eat," I said.

"Anything in particular?"

"Something on rye."

My brother and I had a deep understanding on certain subjects.

"There is a place," he said.

"I knew there would be," I said. "Is it open right now?"

Marlowe took me to to the one and only Jewish deli in Asia. It was run by a lady from New York. Corned beef, kosher pickles and bottles of Dr. Brown's Celery Tonic were flown in twice a week. He told me that the imperial family were big take-out customers, and that Princess Michiko had a heavy gefilte fish habit.

Everything was as it should be. It cost twice what it would have in New York, or twenty times the price of an equivalent meal in 1967 Tokyo—but there was no equivalent.

As I sucked on the half-sour pickle that had been served with my second pastrami on rye, I realized that I had been closer to a critical state than I had realized.

"You saved my life," I said.

"I know," Marlowe said.

I decided it would be safe to stay in Japan for a while. I never went back to the deli. Knowing it was there was enough. Besides, I was investigating the local cuisine.

By day, I photographed Zen temples and acquired works of art. By night, I haunted the noodle shops of Shinjuku. The exchange rate was favorable. A hundred yen amounted to about 28 cents, and for that sum, one such as myself could get a large bowl, with stuff floating—I knew not what it was.

These night-noodle shops were always crowded with other gluttons. I came to like the Japanese people—they appeared to eat constantly. And naturally, they liked me.

It wasn't just noodles. In addition to sushi and tempura—things I already knew about—there were little places specializing in dishes and styles of cooking I'd never seen or heard of. I'd order by pointing to the lifelike displays of plastic food outside every restaurant.

It was a sort of fat guy's heaven.

Of course, this was twenty years ago and more. I've lived through the seventies, and most of the eighties. I've gained knowledge. I've found out that food can hurt you. I live in a town where a deli is a place where you buy olive loaf and potato salad that's delivered by truck. I can't remember the last time I got a sesame seed stuck in my teeth. I don't eat sugar, and I stay away from grease. I've changed since those days in Japan.

The Japanese have changed too. Now they eat gold. Maybe you saw this on the news. Some sushi restaurants are offering tidbits wrapped in gold leaf.

The voice-over narration says the gold doesn't add anything to the taste of the food—just about 40 dollars to the price of the lunch assortment.

The news footage shows suburban Japanese yuppie-types, eating their 24–karat tuna belly. No festivity, no big occasion or celebration—just munching. One guy is reading a comic book. Are these my fellow noodle-slurpers, or their sons?

I'm glad Lafcadio Hearn didn't live to see this.

Arrigato dozai mas, Why Does Everybody Laugh at Us?

When I was in Japan, staying in a student hostel, I took up with a tall guy from Vermont, a Peace Corps volunteer on his vacation. He'd been serving on the island of Puluwat— a remarkable place—but's that's another story, and it's not my story.

This fellow's name was Silverberg, and he was a whiz at Japanese. He told me he had never learned a foreign language until he got in the Peace Corps. They taught him Puluwat. There were only a few hundred speakers of pure Puluwat in the world, and now he was one of them.

His confidence was so high that he actually learned to speak Japanese in twenty-four hours from the book *Learn to Speak Japanese in Twenty-four Hours.* Twenty-four hours was how long it took him to get from Puluwat to Tokyo, and he studied the book the whole way. I had a book, too, and could order food and ask directions. The difference was that Silverberg could understand the responses. I had to rely on pointing and map drawing and pantomime.

Silverberg and I took a train to Kamakura, where the big statue of Buddha is. I had a book about old temples, and there were supposed to be some good ones there. I wanted to see the sort of place Lafcadio Hearn wrote about. There was a real old temple on the edge of town. We took a bus.

45

There were a couple of Japanese girl student-types on the bus, carrying architecture books. Silverberg asked if they knew where we should get off to find this old temple.

They said that was where they were going. We should get off when they did, and follow them. We followed the girls at a respectful distance—so they wouldn't think we were mashers.

The girls went up what looked like a suburban street. We went after them. The suburban street turned into a country road, always rising steadily—we were climbing a hill—keeping the girls' white blouses in view. We hiked for about an hour.

We got to the temple. It was a big disappointment. My guide-book said that the temple no longer operated as such. There was a famous cooking school and restaurant there now, and people came to see an example of an intact monastery of such and such a century. It was really plain. Unimpressive.

"Is this it?" we wondered. Maybe there was more. Something interesting. We wanted a real taste of Zen.

There were the two girls going through a sort of stone archway, like a doorway in the side of a hill. "That must be where it is," we said. We went after them.

Carved into the hillside were stone steps. We started up. It was blazing hot. Mosquitoes stung us. We climbed. The steps went all the way up the hill. About halfway up there was an inscribed rock I liked. I took a picture of it. We kept climbing. Hundreds of steps.

At the top there was a broken down little teahouse, boarded up. There was no view—trees and bamboo had grown up all around the peak too thick to see past. A few feet down the hill, obscured by the foliage, some people were singing. Sounded like kids. That must be where the girls were—the architecture students' picnic maybe. We started down.

By the time we reached the bottom again we were worn out. We stood around in the crummy temple yard, a few chickens walking around. There was a sort of lean-to we hadn't noticed on the way up—a couple of crude benches under it, and an old man.

"You wish tea?" the old man said. His English was perfect, but creaky-sounding.

"Yes. Thank you."

From somewhere the old man came up with a couple of rough, but beautiful bowls. Out of a thermos, he poured hot water, and mixed a green powder into it with a bamboo whisk.

"Sit here," he said, "and look at this bell."

Something else we hadn't noticed. There was an enormous cast bell hanging from a crossbeam. A magnificent and venerable thing.

"This tea is bitter," the old man said. "Here are sweet cakes. Take a tiny bite of the sweet cake, and then sip some tea. Hold the bowl like this."

It was the traditional tea ceremony, of course. They arrange tours for vistors to Japan to see one.

Silverberg and I sat on a bench, and sipped our tea. A little breeze came up from somewhere. We looked at the ancient bell, and saw how perfectly beautiful the old temple really was.

"If you're looking for Zen," the old man said, "you won't find it here. This place has been closed for a hundred years. It's a cooking school now."

We thanked the old man, paid a few yen for our tea and walked away, feeling we'd been there at that old temple forever.

Jambo, Paisan!

Chicago folklore of the nineteen-fifties and 'sixties. In those days, no matter where you went you'd see this message painted or chalked on walls: FREE JOMO KENYATTA. And FREE KENYA EAST AFRICA.

You will remember that the British colonial authorities kept Mzee Jomo Kenyatta under house arrest for a number of years. He was more or less the father of Kenyan independence, and when he got out he became the first president of the Republic of Kenya.

I'm usually a little shaky on dates and details of history, but that's the general picture.

What I want to tell you about is the guy who painted those slogans all over Chicago. To say the least, nobody knew who Jomo Kenyatta was—or where Kenya was. Even less than today.

The guy who painted the slogans was a disabled veteran. I forget his name. It was something like Eddie Matzocci—let's say it was Eddie Matzocci. Eddie was one hundred percent disabled. It was mental. FREE KENYA EAST AFRICA and FREE JOMO KENYATTA were what you call a fixed idea.

In addition to the graffiti, he also left stacks of nearly illegible mimeographed pages in the vestibules of office buildings, libraries and lunchrooms. And he spoke regularly in Bughouse Square.

Bughouse Square was one of the greatest places in Chicago. Newberry Park is the real name. It's about a block square. Bordering it is the Newberry Library, a magnificent research library, open for use by anybody except high school and college students, with, among other things, a rare-book room with stuff like a Shakespeare folio—you can simply ask for it, and they'll bring it to you on a little rubber-tired cart, and you can read it, hold it in your own hands, sniff it. It's some library.

The Mr. Newberry who endowed the library left the park to the city with the provision that anybody might be allowed to speak on any topic at any time without interference. It's the Marble Arch or Union Square of Chicago. Every night maniacs, political activists, poets and preachers would hold forth in Bughouse Square. On summer nights the speeches would go on until two or three in the morning.

The Bughouse Square audience was a tough crowd to please. It was a good school for speakers and debaters. The audience would heckle and razz any speaker who didn't make sense or entertain them. I've seen guys from divinity school rethink their careers after five minutes of trying to preach to the Bughouse Square gang, of whom I was one whenever I got the chance.

Eddie Matzocci was a big favorite of the crowd. He usually wore a rumpled raincoat, and always his American Legion cap. He generally had two shopping bags stuffed with those smeary mimeographed handbills about FREE KENYA EAST AFRICA.

What Eddie offered the crowd was intensity and drama. "This is serious business!" he'd say. "I was shot at the other day on Michigan Avenue! Yeah, a couple of British agents took a shot at me! Those guys are pretty mad about losing their Empire!"

The crowd would always pick up on Eddie's enthusiasm. "Those no-good English!" someone would shout. "Declare war on England! We beat 'em twice before—we can do it again!"

Few people knew that Eddie sent Jomo Kenyatta something

like two dollars and eighty-five cents out of each of his army pension checks—and had done so for years. And he sent him letters of encouragement, reports on the progress of the cause of Kenyan independence in the United States.

So when Kenya was granted independence, they let our State Department know that there was only one American whose credentials they wished to recognize as ambassador. Eddie Matzocci. Seems he was the only American who cared about Uhuru, and they sort of wanted to meet him.

When the State Department finally tracked Eddie down they were—well, sort of disconcerted. To put it mildly, he wasn't ambassadorial material. They wondered if the new government of Kenya had informed Eddie of their intentions, and whether they'd be able to talk him out of accepting the post.

It worked out all right. Eddie didn't want to be ambassador. He wanted to keep doing what he was good at. I was in Chicago maybe ten years after Kenya got independence, and still, printed in letters a foot high all over town, in fresh paint, it said FREE JOMO KENYATTA and FREE KENYA EAST AFRICA.

Henny Oldman

Chicago underground history and folklore. The Chicken Man. He was an old black man in a rumpled raincoat. He used to appear everywhere, like the guy who chalked FREE KENYA EAST AFRICA on walls in every imaginable corner of the city.

I often saw the Chicken Man on the Clark Street bus, on my regular 2 A.M. ride to the Clark Theater, which showed a different double bill every day and cost fifty cents to get in.

In addition to the raincoat, the Chicken Man had a string, like a bandolier, strung across his body diagonally. From the string, various items of junk dangled—tiny beer bottles, a toy telephone, a baby doll. He wore a hat. Under the hat nestled a live white chicken. A trained chicken. When the Chicken Man felt the circumstances were right, he'd doff the hat, and the chicken would hop onto his shoulder and perform.

The chicken danced, clucked into the toy telephone, and drank beer from one of the tiny bottles. The Chicken Man also danced and kept up an unintelligible patter. I don't recall ever seeing him pass the hat. Apparently he was interested in art, not money. He was lean and tall, and could run with a steady loping stride and be out of sight in no time.

People would shout when they saw the Chicken Man, and encourage him to go into his act. He never responded. He was detached, aloof, intent on his art—watching for the moment to set his trained chicken in motion, and the moment to disappear.

You never knew where you'd run into the Chicken Man. I saw him in neighborhoods most people never went to, or even knew existed.

I remember a fellow who went crazy. He had the idea that the chicken act was just a sideline. He believed that the Chicken Man made $75,000 a year, in some other line of work, while he, my friend, couldn't find a job. He talked about the Chicken Man all the time. Finally, my friend made an appointment with a psychiatrist. While he sat in the waiting room before his first appointment, the door to the consulting room opened, and the Chicken Man walked out.

It was more then the crazy guy could take, and he ran out of the office. He didn't stay to find out whether the Chicken Man was a patient, or the doctor.

I wrote about the Chicken Man in a book called *Lizard Music*. I got letters from people who had lived in Chicago. Most of them wanted to tell me that they remembered a Chicken Man like mine, but they remembered him as a product of their imaginations. They hadn't been sure they'd really seen him. The writers of these letters were intrigued that I knew about him too.

My friend, the one who went crazy, got a job driving a cab part-time. He'd come to my door after midnight, and tell me how many times he'd seen the Chicken Man that day. He'd see him maybe five or six times in widely scattered locations. I didn't think he was hallucinating. I myself might see the Chicken Man north of the Loop, and later the same day, near the stockyards, or the university.

There used to be a place north of the Loop called the E. J. Sperry Thought Factory. It was a brownstone house on a quiet corner. Outside, there were bulletin boards, and a sign—E. J. Sperry Thought Factory. There were little scraps of paper tacked to the bulletin boards. Thoughts. Not epigrams, or snatches of poetry. Just thoughts. Some were simple, like *PENCIL*. Or, *DAYLIGHT*. Or, *HUNGRY*. Some were more complicated, verging on the philosophical, like, *Although the moon is smaller than the earth, it is farther away*. I never knew what one was supposed to do with the thoughts. Sometimes I'd take one I liked and put it in my wallet. I still find them used as bookmarks. I never wrote a thought for the bulletin board, although I always wanted to. I just never was able to come up with one when the opportunity was at hand.

For a while there were messages addressed to the Chicken Man. *I see you everywhere*, one said. Another said, *Who are you? You've got to tell me*. And, *Can you help me find a decent job?*

They were obviously written by my friend, the one who went crazy, the one who drove a cab.

As far as I know, the Chicken Man never got in touch with him. I'd be surprised if he had. It wasn't his style.

If Milk Duds Be the Food of Love

The Julian was a neighborhood movie house in Chicago.

On Saturday morning, kids bearing lunch lined up outside the theater. Inside, streaked prints of Hoot Gibson and Ken Maynard unreeled in an atmosphere redolent of Milk Duds and Mason Dots. Empty popcorn boxes flew through the darkness. Mothers prowled up and down the aisles calling the names of unfortunates whose presence was required at home.

It was at the Julian that I was introduced to Sabu, Flash Gordon, and Don Winslow of the Navy.

The Julian was my first experience of culture. An audience made up of kids from various neighborhood and subneighborhoods, pupils in different schools, unknown to one another, would come together and enter communally into a world of darkness and splendor.

Kids being acutely aware of propriety, I quit going to the Julian when I aged out—maybe at 11.

Years later, as a wretched late adolescent, I discovered the Clark Theater.

The Clark was on the backside of the Loop in downtown Chicago. The Clark had a different double bill every 24 hours, and it ran round the clock.

It cost fifty cents to get in if you had a college ID card. They weren't too fussy about identification, and a little pen work on

54

a last year's card belonging to an actual college student would do the trick.

The Clark predated the art movie houses and revival houses that are just now facing extinction. Though the regular audience no doubt included serious students of cinema, most of the people who went there didn't know that word.

People lived there. It was possible to hide in the toilets during the half-hour a day the place was closed in an effort to sweep out squatters. An agile person, homeless or on the lam, could parlay his fifty cents' admission into a week's rent. Hot dogs were sold in the lobby—and popcorn is nutritious. People would make friends there, meet their life partners—undoubtedly, children were conceived.

Most people would hit the Clark at a regular hour. Life in Chicago in those days didn't include much joy for the likes of me and other Clark regulars, and it would have been unthinkable to get through a day without a fantasy fix. I got to have a nodding acquaintance with people whose shift at the Clark ended at 2 A.M. when mine started.

The bills were endlessly varied. There would be the predictable John Wayne Festival, a Marlon Brando double bill, Martin and Lewis—but also things unheard of. I saw the whole Apu trilogy there one night. *Grand Illusion* was paired with some grade B 1950s war movie.

Understand, I didn't know movies were art. They were movies. I'd hardly look at the posters going in. What they had was what I'd see. So I might go in and see *Battleship Potemkin* along with *Killers from the Red Planet*. Or *Seven Samurai* along with *They Drive by Night*.

I saw films there I've never seen (or heard of) again—an actually funny German comedy called *Wir Wunderkinder*. An unintentionally hilarious Japanese movie called *Utamaro, Painter of Women*. *Eroica*—or the Beethoven Story, one of the only movies I've ever walked out of, not because I was dissatisfied: just the opposite. *"Ich habe genug,"* I said, and staggered out into the night.

The most amazing thing that ever happened to me there was the time I walked into a Marx Brothers festival at 2 or 3 A.M. on an arctic February night. The whole city was still—frozen solid. There was hardly an empty seat in the Clark. Harpo had the people going wild. I saw people actually staggering and rolling in the aisles. Strangers pounded each other on the back. The man in front of me turned around in his seat, and grabbed me by the shoulders, and stared into my face, tears of laughter streaming down his cheeks. Pan-Daemonium—the real thing. It's impossible for me to watch the Marx Brothers now—without that audience there's no point—and forget television.

When I was in Chicago a few years ago, the Clark was a porno house—and year before last, I couldn't find it at all.

Sometimes I feel that my whole purpose in life is to tell people who might not have seen it that such a place as the Clark existed. And now I've told you.

Lights! Action! Wingtips!

My uncle Boris claimed to have purchased the first movie camera in Poland to come into private hands. The person selling him the camera had instructed him to always include the feet of his subject, doubtless meaning that Boris should photograph living persons from sufficient distance to show them head-to-toe.

Boris interpreted this differently, and thus came upon what was to be his cinematic signature, the long pan, down the body to the shoes, where the shot lingered.

As Boris's technique expanded, he devised lateral pans of the feet of a number of people sitting on a sofa, tracking shots of the feet of three or four people abreast, walking toward the camera along the sidewalk, and low-angle shots of dancing feet.

Boris completed a feature-length film entitled *Skies 1940*, in which he had spliced together shots of the sky in all 48 states. Some members of the family commented that the film would have been more educational had he labeled each shot according to state. He ignored these Philistine suggestions. The film ended with a Fourth of July parade in Oklahoma or New Jersey—Boris couldn't remember which.

My favorites of Uncle Boris's films were those in which I appeared. There were many reels of me, as a cute little kid, being swung through the air by blue-chinned men in tight-fitting overcoats with wide shoulder pads and snap-brim hats. These were my father, uncles and older brothers—or possibly some of Al Capone's lieutenants.

Actually beautiful was Boris's film *Times Square Nights*, and he made one movie that, I think, was a genuine masterpiece. This was *Berenheimer's Oriental Gardens*.

I've yet to discover where Berenheimer's Oriental Gardens is or was. That it was a real place was demonstrated by the opening shot—of the electric sign flashing the name.

The film consisted mainly of views of exotic flora, bronze replicas of pagodas and water buffalos, and long shots of Boris himself, walking toward the camera. In each shot in which he appears, Boris is dressed in a different outfit, straw hat, hand-painted necktie, spats. He looked like Erich von Stroheim. These shots alternate with closeups of small black-and-white photos, in gold frames, suspended, trembling, among the leaves of some exotic plant. The photos appear to be of persons, but the reflections on the glass of the frame make the images obscure and unrecognizable. These sequences, the foliage, the statuary, Boris, the photographs, are repeated again and again. The film has a dreamlike quality.

But Boris's great work was a collaboration with my father, who was Boris's disciple in the art of cinema, and was himself an exponent of the foot-shot. The two of them converted our dining room into an editing room, and spent a number of weeks cutting all the foot footage out of the family films and splicing them into a two-hour epic entitled *Feet*.

There was no hint they were anything but serious about this project. They would show the film every time they got a chance, excitedly encouraging the viewers to guess whose feet they were looking at. "Look! Whose feets is that? Nah! Wrong! It's Aunt Sadie's feets!" They loved that film. It was an interactive art experience.

Is it any wonder, after growing up on the cutting edge of the cinema avant-garde, that I was not overly impressed when I got to college and was exposed to serious film? I enjoyed the work of Buñuel and Bergman and Dreyer—but after cutting my eye-teeth on the work of my uncle and father, I found it . . . well . . . sort of pedestrian.

PART THREE

FISCHVHISTLE

My Zaydeh Nicotine

When I was twelve or so, I got fanatical about those Sherlock Holmes movies with Basil Rathbone, and then took to reading the stories with even more avidity.

Sherlock Holmes is the ultimate hero for adolescent boys. He's emotionless, cool, knows what he's doing, never gets flustered, never has feelings of insecurity, never gets pimples or spontaneous erections during science class. I suppose Mr. Spock is the modern exponent of the myth. But Spock doesn't have the panache of Holmes, and he doesn't smoke a pipe.

Whenever Holmes and Watson weren't hot on the trail of evil, they were fooling with pipes. The sitting room at 221B was always redolent of latakia. There is hardly a story in which Holmes isn't stinking up the joint with the shag tobacco he kept in that Persian slipper. He couldn't even think without gulping quantities of Escudo, Craven's or Balkan Sobranie. "This is a five-pipe problem, Watson," he'd say, and knock off a whole tin of Navy Cut.

It goes without saying that I took to the pipe as soon as I could. I was fourteen. I made a deal with my father. There was no chance of smoking on the sly. With the father I had, there was no chance of doing anything on the sly. Much like the Great Detective himself, my father used to astound me with detailed accounts of my private activities.

"So, bum! Vhen you vas supposed to be studying in deh library, you vent instead vit' your bum friends, ent vas making a nuisance by deh drugstore!"

"Assuming it's true, how could you have found out?"

"I hev mine methods."

Under the circumstances, I could only apply for official permission to use tobacco. To my astonishment, it was granted— with conditions. I might never use cigarettes, only cigars or a pipe, and only at home.

"Go immediately! Buy a pipe. Here's a dollar."

I knew what he was up to. He was preparing the classic object lesson. I was going to smoke myself sick, and there would be an end to the business.

I flew to the drugstore, and selected a big nasty billiard at fifty-nine cents, from the basket on the counter. Also a pack of Edgeworth, the favorite smoke of Josef Stalin and other men of achievment.

Back in the living room, I loaded the thing up. It must have held an ounce. Holmes could have solved the Sign of Four in two smokes with that footwarmer.

"Sit back. Relax. Have a good smoke, Sonnye." My father was beaming. Soon I had the thing alight, sputtering and gurgling and making clouds of acrid smoke. It burned my eyes and tickled my nose. I loved it.

My father wandered in and out of the living room every few minutes. In between times, I thought I could hear muffled chortling from the kitchen.

"So? How do you like it?" he would say. "You know who you look like vit' det pipe? Albert Einstein!" Then he would bolt for the kitchen again.

I stuck with it. The bowl of the pipe was getting hot, and the varnish was bubbling. My tongue was beginning to feel like a Brillo pad.

"Vhat? You finished it? Smoke another one. Use up deh tobacco vhile it's still fresh."

I looked him straight in the eye, and charged the pipe, which was now getting foul and soggy. "This is great, Dad," I said.

"Smells vonderful too," my father said.

It was a battle of wills. I smoked seven pipefuls of Edgeworth, while my father encouraged me.

One really does turn sort of green in such a situation. I noticed that in the bathroom mirror, when I lurched in to run cold water on my tongue. One also gets horribly dizzy.

However, I did not stagger or fall to the floor. And I never copped out that I didn't love the experience.

A week later, I visited the English Pipe Shop on Monroe Street, and bought a Peterson Prince of Wales, which I have to this day.

My father was beaten—hoist with his own petard. His logic had been sound, but he hadn't counted on the power of a fictional hero. If Holmes could handle shag, I could deal with Edgeworth.

If I ever come down with cancer I'm going to sue the estate of Sir Arthur Conan Doyle.

On First Looking into
Kurtzman's *Mad*

Much have I travell'd in the realms of gold. And many goodly jokes and cartoons seen.

There was a huge newsstand on a side street, just off Hollywood Boulevard. It was close to half a block long—one of those places where you could get out-of-town newspapers, and magazines in foreign languages. Naturally, they had the best selection of comic books in town.

I was maybe ten years old. I was with my mother. She was doing some shopping, and I had to go along with her. We stopped at the newsstand. She told me I could pick out one comic book. Then we were going to some lady restaurant for lunch.

So I stood there, scanning the comic book section. And there it was. *Mad* comics. I'd never seen it before. Never heard of it. It was brand new. I was looking at *Mad* number one—the very first issue. In later years, *Mad* changed its format, and became the black-and-white humor magazine on sale today. In the beginning, it was a full-color comic book. Fifty-two pages. It cost a dime.

It was astonishing. The art was like nothing I'd ever seen. It was funny art. It was good art, too—but I didn't know about things like that yet. The stories were parodies of other comic books. "Superduperman" was one. There was a story called

"Ganefs," about a couple of crooks. There was a wonderfully ugly character called The Mole.

I stood there in the street, transfixed. Like stout Cortez with eagle eyes, I stared at the drawings of Bill Elder and Wally Wood.

It was irreverent. It was crude. The humor was overdone, high-energy, laugh-a-minute, nothing sacred. In later years, I would encounter other exponents of the pandaemonic style: the Marx Brothers, "The Goon Show," Monty Python, and the book review section of *The New York Times*. I felt as though I had discovered a new planet. This comic was drawn and written just for me.

If you ever loved *Mad* in its present incarnation, and were born too late to see the original comic, I can only pity you. For better or worse, whatever sort of writer I am today has a lot to do with those vulgar masterpieces I devoured in the 'fifties.

I knew a kid, named Mark Roughborough, in junior high school who had two subscriptions to *Mad*. Avid as I was, this dumbfounded me. Why have two subscriptions to the same comic? It seemed a waste of money.

"One of them I read," Mark told me. "The other, I take out of the envelope only once, to check that it's in perfect condition. I keep those copies in this file cabinet."

"But why? Why do that?"

"I don't know. I just do it. I think these comics might be valuable someday."

He was so right. By the time he was ready to go to college, Mark could have easily paid for his first year with what his collection of *Mad*s was worth. And bought a car.

My own complete run of *Mad*, from number one to the abandonment of the full-color format, I loaned to Leo Kratzner on a Friday afternoon.

The next Monday, he wasn't in school. "Where's Leonard?" I asked the teacher.

"His mother took him out of school. They've moved to Connecticut."

The slimy little wretch.

Listen, Kratzner. Maybe you're reading this. I want my comics. Don't think you've gotten away with it. Sooner or later, I'll catch up with you.

It would be better for you, Kratzner, if you came forward of your own free will, instead of sitting silent, upon a peak in Darien.

Rhapsody in Glue

I can remember a time when a boy, hearing an airplane, might run out of the house and peer into the sky, his hand shading his eyes. Other boys too would call to one another and look upward at the colored object. We were little boys. Some of us might not be entirely clear as to what an airplane was, but I remember that the sight of one was thrilling.

(Looking up) "There! There it is!"

"Yep. It sure is!"

"Yep."

"It's way up there!"

"Yep."

I grant that we were not expert in conversation, but we knew what we meant. We meant that the object was beautiful. At the age of five, in my neighborhood, it would have been considered unmanly to say it. Lash LaRue would not have said it. Hopalong Cassidy would not have said it. We were already learning to be inarticulate louts, but the tiny machine in the sky stirred our souls, and evoked an emotion we were years away from acknowledging in connection with females. It was a combination of admiration and yearning, which was accompanied by a need to pretend we knew what we were talking about.

"That's a mail plane," one might say, and the others would all agree.

69

Or, "That's a German plane" (we were at war), and we would
then narrow our eyes and project hatred upward.

The fact of airplanes constituted a mystery. It was part of the
secret kid subculture that flourished then, and is thought not to
flourish so much now, but does. I don't recall, in those days,
helpful adults who brought us out of the darkness of mythopoeic
thought and primitive ritual. We were taught a standard curric-
ulum at school, what manners and morals seemed essential at
home, and were otherwise on our own a good deal. I was and
am grateful for this adult neglect, given that the culture of the
backyards was as rich as it was, and for the first eight or nine
years developed along the lines of the less progressive natives
of New Guinea.

Those very natives, I believe, are the world's most ardent
model-airplane builders. Their models, which are full-scale or
at least large, are intended to work as decoys of a sort, to bring
cargo-laden planes to earth in their part of the jungle. Anyway
that is what they told the anthropologists. I can only report what
I know from watching educational TV.

There is something to be said for the sympathetic-magic theory
of model-building. The Paleolithic cave painters drew "models"
of animals they hoped to encounter. The New Guineans may
well have fashioned airplanes in hopes of getting the contents
of one—or just making the distant thing come close. I build a
model of a portion of my childhood, and as I do so it becomes
momentarily vivid, almost graspable.

What I am saying here is that model-building is a basic
inclination, particularly of primitive man, which includes all
boys.

I suppose some girls built models, even then—and modern
convention requires that I mention them now—but in truth,
females hardly existed in the Papuan jungle I inhabited in the

nineteen-forties and the beginning of the 'fifties. Objects of love, desire and frustration were made of balsa wood and tissue paper.

I recently visited a hobby shop, and what I saw made me profoundly sad. All the boxes of unassembled wonders contained pieces of plastic! There were a few models, suspended on wires from the ceiling—but these had the aspect of museum pieces. They were relics of decades past. The modern model-builder snaps together injection-molded parts, sometimes not even requiring the application of glue. The skill is in the painting of the finished project—occupational therapy for idiots—this was merely the last stage of the process when I was a Neanderthal nipper.

The equivalent of the plastic model kit, for us, was the "solid" model. Depending on price, this might consist of a partially formed fuselage, requiring a good deal of sanding and shaping— or, in the super economy class, a simple block, which the young craftsman was supposed to carve with his X-Acto knife. Paper templates were supplied, which were supposed to be glued to cardboard and cut out, and applied to the fuselage and wings to achieve the proper contours. While looked down upon as a diversion for little kids, these solid jobs were actually impossible to build, and the results never looked like anything but potatoes with wings. To compound the frustration, the devils who made up these kits included glue in the form of powder in an envelope, which when mixed with water, produced something of the consistency of Swiss health-cereal with the sticking power of thin air. Insignia were printed in two or, if you were lucky, three colors on the sheet of paper with the templates and confusing instructions. The idea was to cut out the insignia and, in a last-ditch effort to make the pathetic thing look like an airplane, stick them on with the same horrible lumpy paste.

Once upon a time, some early lowbrow discovered that he

could jam his favorite rock into the end of a cleft stick, and thereby increase the arc and velocity with which he could get his food, and gain the respect of his neighbors. It was much the same when I came upon Testor's model airplane cement (eventually replaced by the revolutionary quick-drying variety, the experience of which innovation prepared me emotionally to later enter the computer age without missing a beat). With the magical ambroid, I was able to keep the solid models from falling apart as I built them, and at the age of seven or eight, I not only made a putative Grumman Wildcat with both wings attached, but glued everything I owned to everything else I owned, with satisfying results.

It was a short step from Testor's cement to Testor's model airplane dope, and the abandonment of watercolors. The finished product still looked like a potato, but the parts remained stuck on, and the paint looked shiny and good. I was on the high road to craftsmanship.

Craftsmanship was embodied in the "stick" model. These kits came in boxes looking much like the boxes spaghetti comes in— and contained a multitude of thin strips of balsa wood, looking much like spaghetti, sheets of thin balsa, imprinted with a variety of curious shapes, a folded sheet of tissue paper, and a sheet of plans.

Newspaper would be spread on the dining room table, with admonishments from Mother about what the fate would be of a boy who got a single drop of glue on the finish. On top of the newspaper a sheet of cardboard would be placed, on top of the cardboard the sheet of plans, and over that, waxed paper—all held in place with tape or pins. This was the assembly stage for the airplane, contained as an ideal image within the box of wood products and the mind of the aspirant.

The shapes printed on the sheet of balsa would have numbers of designation printed on them, and represented fuselage bulkheads, wing spars, and other components. These shapes, which mostly appeared as concentric ovals, rectangles and crescents of various sizes, had square notches around their perimeters. With single-edged razor blade, or trusty X-Acto knife, the model maker would cut these out, with infinite care.

The highest grade of kit had precut components, but who could afford such luxury? The notches were the places where the balsa stringers would be glued, held in place with pins until the glue was dry.

The wings were built directly on the plans, the spars, like little chips, positioned on double lines, each labeled with the number of the spar. As the wings took shape on the waxy surface, pins bristling, the aspect of the thing became like a dissection tray, with the skeleton of some improbable creature being, in this case, not taken apart, but put together.

And the whole shaky, amazing, fragile and desperate enterprise would have to be shifted from the table when supper was ready.

I don't recall ever being taught any of these techniques—that is to say, no kindly or professional adult ever sat me down and explained how to build a model airplane. The skills were picked up from reading the instructions that came with the airplanes— some through trial and error, some from conversation, or glimpses of some other kid's model-in-progress. My elder brother certainly gave me some tips, having "built his model."

Which brings me to the consideration of this topic, which I find most interesting. I never regarded building models as a hobby. I know that some do, and no doubt people who were kids in school with me are building them to this day—but for me, and for most kids I knew, it was something you did for a time, and with a sort of goal in mind. The goal was not clearly defined, but it would be the point at which you could quit building the things. This tended to coincide with adolescence taking a good hold—but ideally it would also be at a point marked by the creation of a masterpiece, or masterpieces. That accomplished, you could hand down your venerable piece of chipboard to a younger kid, and move on toward manhood.

My own unsurpassable ultimate was the creditable completion of a Fokker Dr-I triplane from a twenty-five-cent Comet kit. These kits were the cheapest on the market, and they were execrable things. For your quarter you got a tiny spaghetti box containing a sheet of splintery, frangible balsa, murkily printed in blue with fuselage cross-sections and wing formers, tiny blue blobs indicating the notches to be cut out for the stringers. The stringers themselves were not precut, but had to be sliced out of another sheet of balsa, as tricky and crumbly as the first. The plans looked as though they might be the work of Albrecht Dürer in his solid-model days.

This was the ultimate challenge. The over-the-shoulder mirror shot at six clay pigeons. Only a brand-new razor blade, and careful study of the grain of the wood, would permit the cutting out of the parts without the horrible material disintegrating. To save the cost of a second sheet of newsprint, the makers had printed plans and instructions in a fiendishly tiny, compacted and abbreviated fashion on something no larger than a sheet of notebook paper. The actual model, if it could somehow be completed, was to be a dazzlingly small miniature—the Lord's Prayer written on a grain of rice, the boy Mozart's violin. I was pretty sure no one had ever put one of these together.

There are moments when you know you are ready. With absolute certainty, I laid out my portable studio on the dining room table.

I entered into a state of samadhi. My mind was clear—I was resolute. I rose above the seething turmoil of family life. Parents, siblings, pets, all merged into an unobtrusive murmur some distance away. I was calm. I was prepared. To focus my meditative state, I employed the old Hindu trick of listening to the radio. Bob and Ray and X Minus One provided mantras as I worked.

Days at school were dreamlike, serene. I did not get involved. I was saving my strength for the great work taking place at home.

It went perfectly! The delicate skeletons of wings, tail and fuselage were constructed, and assembled. The undercarriage went on—the tail skid. It was complete, the skeleton. It was beautiful.

It is said that artists love their sketches better than their finished paintings. I once saw an X ray of a Rembrandt underpainting, and the master had laid the foundation for his picture by putting down darks and light in what looked to me like a first-class abstract expressionist work. I wonder if he took a day to admire it before he obscured the vigorous brushstrokes to make an image suitable to the conventions of his time.

Some model-builders—grown ones with plenty of money—were given to covering their models with clear acetate instead of tissue paper, to show off the excellence of the structure. Rembrandt and I knew that this parading of craft was vulgar and a violation of the rules of Art.

The tissue paper supplied with the kit was precisely enough to cover the finished airplane—there wasn't a square inch to spare. Careful cutting was called for. Glue was applied to the edges of the wings, for example, and the paper was smoothed on, tucked and trimmed. The paper skin sagged and bulged, suggesting the old potato specter—but this was a temporary phase. After the paper was applied and the glue was dry, the whole surface of the model was to be sprayed with water. The water would dry, and the paper would shrink taut. Instructions with models suggested the use of a perfume atomizer, or an L-shaped device through which one blew, the other angle of the L drawing water from a glass. But the only method I had ever seen employed was the mouth-spritz, such as ironers use. This, one practiced in the bathroom, or on one's little brother, until a fine even spray could be produced.

The last stage—the only stage for the wretched modern plastic model assembler—was the putting on of paint. This was sheer joy for me. The German airplanes of World War One displayed a lot of style when it came to color, and most of the Fokkers were bright red—which was what had interested me in the little triplane to begin with. Now I got to smooth the rich red paint onto the tissue, which had shrunken to follow every contour of the structure. Two coats! And black for the details. When the dope was dry, the thing gleamed.

And it looked and no doubt smelled not much different from the full-size original on the day it came from the factory—and it could fly! Not that much of a flight would ever be ventured with such a treasure—but a tentative shove would send it aloft, eagerly—and a single test glide was undertaken in the living room. It even landed itself, rolling to a stop as though the Red Baron himself were at the stick.

I may have built one or two models after that—but they did not signify. I knew or sensed that I would never experience such a feeling of triumph again. I had earned my wings—three of them.

Fischvhistle

My father spoke no known language. "Mine Yinglisch iz atrootzgious," he would say. An understatement.

He'd started out speaking Polish—I guess. When I went with him to Warsaw one bitter winter in the early sixties, I saw him confound the Poles by speaking to them in what he regarded as their common native tongue.

He could also murder Russian, Yiddish, and German. One theory is that at one time he could speak *something* in standard fashion, but forgot that language while failing to learn—better to say, making up his own version—of new ones.

However, I came to believe that he had always communicated with no regard to anyone else's rules of grammar, diction or syntax. This would be in keeping with the way he did everything.

This is not to say that he could not be understood. One generally knew what he was talking about—but one didn't know how one knew. This could be unsettling.

At times, especially when he waxed (or vexed) philosophical or speculative, the meaning might be elusive. My brother and I made a hobby of deciphering his pronouncements.

Once he said:

Sonnye, I vant you should inwent a fischvhistle.

So vhan you blawink deh fisch vhistel, come deh fisch. Azoy vhan you callink ah cow, compass, compass, compass.

Out with the pencils and paper, and to the kitchen table, to work it out, my brother and I. This was actually an easy one.

What he had said was:

Son, I want you to invent a fish whistle.

When you blow the whistle, fish will come. (simple so far) As when you call a cow, Come Bossy, Come Bossy, Come Bossy.

I have to give my brother credit for that one. "Come Bossy" from "Compass" was an inspiration. If it had been up to me, I'd still be trying to figure it out—like so many things my father told me.

There Are Strange Things Done
'neath the Midnight Sun

Lord Buckley said, "Fate takes its cut." You can't escape destiny. Take my friend Bob Winston, for example.

I met Bob in high school. I went to a big high school in Chicago. It was the first day of the semester, in Mrs. Macintosh's English class. Mrs. Macintosh was an enthusiastic anti-Semite. She used to lecture her classes about how the Jews were sneakily taking over society. Teachers had a lot more freedom to express themselves in those days. The first day of class, all the Jewish kids who had them, and all the Christian kids who could borrow them, would wear little Stars of David around their necks. We'd been told by kids who'd had her the term before how an expression of horror would creep over Mrs. Macintosh's face.

So there I am, sitting in the back row, wearing my Star of David, and Bob Winston comes in late. A beefy kid with a bad haircut, he tripped on the way in.

"Poor guy, he looks half-witted," I thought to myself. "I'll be nice to him."

He sat down in the seat next to me. Much later, I found out that his first thought on seeing me was "Poor guy, he looks half-witted. I'll be nice to him."

We became good friends, and had a number of adventures together through high school and part of college. Then, as happens, he went his way and I went mine.

Actually we went the same way in one respect. We both got fatter. I got a bit fatter. Bob got a whole lot fatter. We're about the same size now. Similar to a walrus.

Bob resents being fat. He worries about it. I think that's a mistake. I've read the statistics, and know what sort of chance I've got of becoming svelte. Not worth mentioning. Bob is a gambler. Long shots appeal to him. He keeps trying.

But like me, he tried and failed at all the conventional and unconventional things you can do to reverse your blimpitude. He's smart. He knows the usual stuff doesn't work. So he's had to fall back on exotic schemes he works out himself. Through the years, he's gotten in touch with me from time to time, usually to discuss his plans for trimming down to the lithe 235 pounds he weighed in high school.

This time he hit upon a magnificent scheme. He decided that his downfall was the availability of really good nosh that can be delivered to your door 24 hours around the clock in Chicago. Bob had only to reach for the phone, and a steady stream of ribs, chicken, state-of-the-art pizzas, Chinese dumplings, and pastrami sandwiches would be brought to his waiting gullet.

So he took a job in Alaska. In a tiny Upik Eskimo village. They needed a schoolteacher—Bob's a schoolteacher. He applied. They hired him. No "24 hour—we deliver" where he was going. Besides, he reasoned, the cold climate would help him burn calories.

He had a fair amount of time on his hands once he got up there, so I heard from him fairly regularly. It was going pretty well at the beginning—and he had lots of interesting information to share. For example, I learned that the Upik Eskimo word for a white person is *gussik*—comes from Cossack—remember, the Russians were there first. And *cheechako*, meaning tenderfoot, a word I know from Jack London stories and old movies, is a

Upik corruption of Chicago. Bob was getting into the local culture. And he was losing weight.

Second or third time I heard from him, he told me about moose stew, and Ah-goo-duk—or eskimo ice cream. It's made of berries, sugar, and Crisco mixed together. He said it was surprisingly good.

I knew it. The diet went to hell. It turned out there was just about nothing the Eskimos eat that he didn't like. That's my point. You can't escape destiny.

Bob's still up there. He likes it. Says the cold doesn't bother him. Another case of a boyhood in Chicago preparing one to survive and thrive anywhere in the world. If the English had deep-dish pizza they could have kept their empire.

You Can Lead a Cow to Quarters

When I was a freshman in college I knew this guy. He was a senior, and he had a car. Fred Lester was his name. We had a symbiotic relationship. I paid for cheeseburgers, and he drove me around. Cheeseburgers were what we had in common. The college was out in the country, surrounded by fields. It was handy to have a friend who had a car.

This college I went to is about the most beautifully situated place I've ever seen. Coming from Chicago, and hardly ever having been in the country, let alone the hills and mountains and forests of the Hudson River valley in upstate New York, I was continually astonished and distracted by scenery. I eventually came to live in this valley, and I still haven't gotten over it—especially in fall. Fall in Chicago, which I liked well enough, is when leaves turn brown. Here—well, you have to see it.

I was drunk on color my first semester at college. I couldn't get much work done. I spent all my time wandering in the woods, and riding around in search of cheeseburgers with Fred Lester. When it got to be Indian summer, and all that splendor combined with balmy weather—and I discovered I could get real live girls to go walking in the woods with me—I was good for nothing. I just stumbled around staring and marveling, and strolling, and flunking out.

One afternoon, Fred Lester found me seated under a tree, gazing at nature.

"Want to come for a ride?" he asked me.

"I haven't got any money," I said.

"No. No cheeseburgers this time. Just come for a ride."

I got in his car. It was an old Plymouth. We drove along a road that bordered the college. On the other side of the road there was a field with cows in it.

Lester stopped the car. "Pick out a cow," he said.

"Pick out a cow?"

"Yes. Pick one you like."

A strange request, but I've always had a taste for nonsense. "That one there."

"Which one?"

"That one there. The brown one. Three cows from the tree."

"That's the cow you like?"

"Sure. I like that cow."

"OK, your choice of cow is noted. I'll drive you back to campus now. It's nearly time for supper."

He drove me back. When I got out of the car, he indicated a coil of rope on the back seat. "See? I've got some rope," he said.

"So you have," I said.

"See you around," he said.

"Right. So long, Fred," I said.

There was a women's dorm not far from the road where Fred had asked me to pick out a cow.

Later that night, I heard that a cow had been discovered wandering on the second floor. Everybody was at supper except Edith Cranford, a philosophy major who was in her room, drinking. When Edith came out of her room she saw the cow.

"Moo," the cow said.

Edith went back into her room, and began to cry softly. She tended to see pathos in things.

It turns out that cows can go up stairs, but not down stairs. A veterinarian had to be called, and the cow tranquilized and lowered to the ground in a sling. No harm came to the cow.

Everybody wondered who had done it. The administration wanted to expel the culprit.

I never said a word about it to anyone.

I had picked out the cow, and been shown the rope it would be led with. I was an accessory before the fact.

There's no point doing a prank if there isn't someone who knows you've done it. Fred had his audience, and someone to tell the tale—as I'm doing now.

Fred refused to discuss the incident with me.

Fred was a pre-law student.

You can't be too careful who you ride around in cars with.

Hoopla!

My father was the last person to try to make a fortune in hula hoops in the 1950s.

Enough time has gone by that there will be some who don't know what a hula hoop was. It was a hoop made of extruded plastic tubing, semirigid, maybe four feet in diameter. The idea was to twirl it around your body by gyrating your hips. It was a national craze.

My father got into hula hoops late. He press-ganged me into being the manufacturing side of the business. He took me to a warehouse-like room. There were enormous piles of lengths of plastic tubing, ready to make into hoops. I was supposed to grab a length of tubing, insert a short wooden plug halfway into one end, bend the tubing around, insert the other half of the plug into that, and then fit the newly made hoop into a stapling machine that worked by a foot pedal— shoot staples into both sides of the plug, through the plastic, and toss the hoop onto the pile of finished items.

I made a lot of hula hoops. Problem was, by this time, everybody who was going to buy a hula hoop had bought one. And it was a bulky item. A box containing a dozen hula hoops was a pretty big box. They sold for maybe a dollar, dollar and a half. The cost of shipping ate up the profit.

For years after, my father would say to me, "Sonnye, tink of somp'in else to do vit' dose hoops."

Somebody—not my father—made millions in the hula hoop business. It had been the same thing with yo-yos in the forties. These fads come along of themselves, it seems. But people are always trying to precipitate them—having gotten a lock on the market in advance.

I have been told, a number of times, how from pop art on, all movements in American art have begun with photocopied sheets of specifications generated by certain gallery owners and museum curators, and sent to selected artists. The spec sheets tell the artist what to make and how to make it.

When I graduated from college—an art major—pop art had just hit. One of my professors was an insider from New York. He gave me a hot tip.

"Retinal art," he whispered out of the corner of his mouth.

"Retinal art?" I asked him.

"Hurts the eye. Lots of tiny stripes. Orange next to blue. It's the next big thing."

Sure enough, the following year, the Museum of Modern Art had the Responsive Eye show—and we had op art for a while.

I've never seen one of those sheets of instructions for making neo-anti-imagist-post-modern painting, but I have seen their equivalent from publishers who put out genre fiction.

And lately, the practice seems to have become common in areas other than mass-produced romances, westerns and science fiction.

Used to be, my agent might say, "I had lunch with such-and-such a publisher. They like your work, and they'd be interested in seeing something you've written." Now she might say, "I had lunch with such-and-such a publisher. They have a book they'd be interested in having you write, and they want to know if they should send the outline over."

It seems a bizarre way to go about things, doesn't it? But it's just people trying to come up with the next hula hoop. Just the traditional attempt to subordinate art to business. Only maybe it's being worked a little harder these days.

It's my contention that many of these synthetic efforts won't endure. The products seldom rise above cleverness, and often they're real boring.

My father did not learn his lesson after the hula hoop fiasco. One day, he handed me an object made of bent coat-hanger wire, forming a sort of loopy double S. It had a plastic handle, like a pistol, and there was a Ping-Pong ball trapped between the two wire S's.

"Loin to play vit dis," he said.

"What is it?"

"It's deh Trickee-Track. It'll be deh nex' yo-yo. Loin to woik it. You'll got to demonstrate it."

The idea was to make the Ping-Pong ball do upside-down loops by flipping the apparatus around. I believe I am the only person who ever became proficient in operating the Trickee-Track. It fizzled in the marketplace.

For all I know, the Trickee-Tracks, in their colorful cartons, are stacked to this day in the corner of some warehouse—along with the thousands of lengths of colorful tubing that never made hula hoops—piled high, like a whole bunch of minimalist sculptures.

Pyrotechnudnik

This is about revenge. It still makes me happy when I think about it.

There was this schmuck in my college dorm. Bill Buehler was his name. A big, noisy, thick-headed lout.

Late at night, when people were sleeping, he'd come in drunk, singing at the top of his lungs. He also had a bugle. He played bugle calls in the stairwell. He also frequently threw up on the stairs, and left his mess for others to clean up.

For a while Bill attached himself to the civil rights movement, I think because they more or less tolerated him. He would have been just as happy as a Nazi. Happier—they had more songs that sounded good with a bugle. Until they threw him out, he made a couple of trips south, ostensibly to demonstrate, with the local student organization. He apparently was a horrible liability, and did nothing on those trips but buy up fireworks, which he'd bring back to college.

After his career as a political activist, Bill had a good stock of explosives to alternate with singing, bellowing, bugling and vomiting.

One night in early spring, I was sitting on the steps when someone dumped a wastebasket full of water out an upstairs window, on my head. Someone. I can still hear that idiotic laugh.

I made a note to destroy him when I got the chance.

The last week of term. People studying for exams, writing term papers. For once it was really quiet in the dorm. Except for the click of typewriters behind closed doors, silence.

Bill Bueheler had rediscovered his love of firecrackers, and had been setting them off all day. Several individuals and deputations had visited him and explained, graphically, how unwise it would be for him to set off any more. Bill was affable. He understood. He promised. He'd stay quietly in his room leafing through his collection of *Playboy* magazines. Bill was not going to be back next semester. No point in starting to study now.

His room was diagonally across from mine. When I heard him leave for the showers, singing sotto voce, I stepped across and helped myself to two healthy-looking firecrackers from the pile on his desk.

I resumed work on my term paper.

Sometime after midnight, I touched the fuse of one of the little darlings to the end of my Camel cigarette, and dropped it out the window. It was a good one.

Immediately, there was a thunder of feet, as many students crowded into Bill Bueheler's room. I heard them describe to him what they would do to his hoard of fireworks, his complete set of *Playboy* magazines, and his worthless carcass should he explode just one more. Of course, they ignored him when he swore he was innocent.

I waited about an hour and sent the second firecracker out into the night.

What happened to Bill Buehler and his prized possessions doesn't bear thinking about. But I do think about it to this day. Suffice it to say that nothing was left untouched.

The next day, I ran into him.

"Pinkwater, I want to thank you," he said. "You're the only guy in the dorm who didn't participate in that massacre last night. Wasn't it horrible what they did to me?"

"Well, Bill," I said, "boys will be boys."

Knits the Ravell'd Pastrami of Care

At the end of the hall, in my college dormitory was the room of Harold Glasgow.

Harold Glasgow had not a single enemy. The mere mention of his name caused people's faces to soften. He was universally loved. His opinion was respected, his approval sought.

He was like a heroic upperclassman in one of those stories about English public schools.

Harold Glasgow had achieved this golden reputation while habitually sleeping no less than eighteen hours a day.

Harold's friends would gather quietly in his room after midnight. He would be in bed, a beautiful expression on his face. They would sit, smoking, talking quietly, watching Harold sleep. He was a genius at it.

Since those days, I have visited vast wildernesses, cloisters, a Zen monastery in Japan—never have I known a place of such tranquility as Harold Glasgow's room.

At one or two, Harold would awaken. He would smile, greet his guests, and engage in conversation of exquisite wit for an hour or so.

Sometimes, one might go to Harold's room during the day, and borrow a book while he slumbered. He had a large collection of light reading—authors like Kingsley Amis, S. J. Perelman and Jerome K. Jerome.

As the rest of us wandered off to bed, Harold, wearing his pajama top as a shirt, would go to his car, a '59 Chevy with a monstrous mobile short-wave outfit in it. He would drive the hundred miles to New York City, communicating with amateur radio operators in foreign lands.

In the city, he would go to Katz's delicatessen, open all night, and famous for the sign SEND A SALAMI TO YOUR BOY IN THE ARMY. He would dine, and drive back to college, chatting with friends on the other side of the planet. To his friends at college, he would bring knishes, and pastrami on rye.

It took three semesters of failure to get bounced out of my college, and with classes inconveniently scheduled during hours of daylight, Harold finally got expelled. He took it with good grace. We helped him load his car, and saw him off. He drove away in the direction of Boston—the ten-foot whip antenna flailing—in the middle of the night.

Years later, I heard that Harold had invited a number of his college friends to visit him at the Plaza Hotel in New York. He had rented a suite. His friends found a handsome buffet, catered by Katz's, and snacked and talked while Harold napped in one of the bedrooms.

As I speak these words, somewhere, Harold is sleeping— doing no harm, generating goodwill—sleeping the sleep of the just and the innocent. How many of us will sleep like that tonight?

Like Mama Never Made

My father admired a guy by the name of Aaron Lebedeff. He was a Yiddish theater performer, a snappy dresser and the inventor of scat-singing and Danny Kaye. His big number was "Rumania, Rumania," which started out with the words "Oh, Rumania, Rumania"—and went on to list all the things you could get to eat there. Some of his other popular songs were "Odessa Mama," which was about food you might get in Odessa, "Gib Mir Bessarabia," about food in Bessarabia. He also did love songs with lines like "Her cheeks are nice and red, just like ripe tomatoes. And she alone is sweet like herring and potatoes."

Apparently the immigrant audiences liked nostalgic songs about places they'd been and things they'd eaten. Half the stuff Lebedeff sang about I've never come across. To my knowledge, I've never eaten *mamalige* as such, and I think *brinze* is cream cheese, but I'm not sure.

My mother was a lousy cook, and on top of that my father had what was referred to as a delicate stomach. He lived on tea, beet borscht, and lean meat. I used to whine that there was no reason that normal meals should not be prepared for those of us who were normal people.

"Ha! You vill yeet vat you fadder yeets!" my father would

say. "Vhen I vas a boy, deh fadder ate vhite bread and us children ate black bread."

Whatever he'd eaten in Poland, it had apparently ruined his digestion—but there was no arguing with him. I'd chew on my burned-to-a-crisp liver, and my green salad with salt *or* pepper—never both.

Where I live nowadays, in the country, you occasionally run into tree-dwellers who believe there's an international Jewish conspiracy. There is one. It's the utter fiction Jews put forth that their mothers could cook.

No wonder those immigrants used to crowd into theaters on Second Avenue to hear Lebedeff sing—not about home cooking—but the delicatessens they'd left behind.

One winter night, I found myself in Paris with my father. In his old age he had conceived a desire to make a trip to Warsaw, and I went with him to carry his bags. He'd given me exactly twenty-four hours' notice, and now with an emergency instant-issue passport, there I was in Paris overnight, en route.

"I'll take you to a real Jewish restaurant," my father said.

"How do you know about a Jewish restaurant in Paris?" I asked him.

"I hoid about it."

We took a taxi to a dingy place in what looked like an industrial section. Inside there were a few tables, a tile floor, and the owner, who looked more or less like my father—mean, bald-headed, small, strong-looking. They peered at each other like a couple of vultures.

I've got no idea in what language or languages this exchange took place, but I got the drift of it:

"Don't I know you from Warsaw?"

"Yeh, you look familiar."

My father was something of a sport in the old days, was said to have been a tough guy, and there was a story that his fare to

America had been raised by subscription. The proprietor of the restaurant looked like he had thrown a few punches in his day too. These guys were remembering each other from forty years before.

"Well. You come to eat?"

"Vhy not?"

Remember, my father had that delicate stomach. In the time I'd known him he'd never eaten anything more exciting than a corn muffin.

I was horrified at what then took place. An eight-course meal. The restaurant guy joined us, and matched my father course for course.

First there was scalding hot chicken soup—minimum fifty percent fat. Delicious.

Chopped liver, glistening with schmaltz. My father inhaled it.

Third was some kind of herring. I dropped out after that. I knew another bite would kill me. Roast chickens followed. Carps' heads, jellied calves' feet, stuff I'd never seen before. The two old guys worked steadily. They took on more cholesterol than the average Greenland Eskimo gets in a month.

They both lived through it. Afterward, my father and I were in the street. He was chewing a toothpick.

"Dat vas good Jewish cooking," he said. "Don't tell your mudder ve vent here."

Honorable Foxy Grandma

During World War Two, various people lived in our house. My father would bring them home and they'd stay for a year or two. The one I remember best was Sonia, a Polish anthropologist. She and her husband lived in the back bedroom for a long time.

That's why I was brought up on Japanese cooking. Sonia was doing a project for the War Department. She was studying Japanese culture with an eye toward coming up with some good ideas for psychological warfare. Sonia did most of the cooking for the family while she lived with us, and to keep in the mood, she prepared a Polish person's idea of Japanese meals.

She was also studying for her American doctorate, and was reviewing physical anthropology. The sort of mental snapshot of Sonia most people in my family remember is that of her, stirring a big pot of miso soup while looking at a textbook propped on the back of the stove, and holding a gorilla skull. Her husband, coming upon this scene, pretended to faint.

I don't know what Sonia's husband did, but he could type long manuscripts while smoking a cigarette and carrying on an unrelated conversation, which impressed me as a little kid.

After getting deeply into Japanese ethnology, Sonia came up with the following interesting facts, and wrote them up for the

96

War Department: it seems that in Japan, foxes are creatures of ill omen, and equate with ghosts. Sonia's idea was to dye a whole bunch of foxes white, transport them to the Japanese mainland, and set them loose in the countryside.

This would demoralize the Japanese populace, who would then overthrow the militarist clique and sue for peace.

In later years, given that our government had fallen back on the atomic bomb, I assumed that Sonia's suggestion had been dismissed.

But recently, I became aware of an unverified story that in the early 'forties a navy submarine had turned a bunch of foxes loose on Long Island. The foxes had been allowed to swim the last hundred yards, the white paint pretty much washed off, and the foxes apparently blended into the countryside and made a living among the many duck farms that used to exist there. It was a nice try, though.

Sonia moved to New York City, and I used to visit her there once in a while. She had gotten interested in those mountain-dwelling Russians—the ones who live into their hundreds, and ride horseback every day—remember them from the yogurt commercials? She was comparing them to another pocket of very old people—on some island in Maine. She wanted to find out how come they all lived so long and what the two groups had in common.

Of course, it turned out that they all smoked, ate fatty foods, drank alcohol and had awful dispositions.

What the two groups had in common, it seems, is that they were terribly interested in local doings and gossip. They'd never leave their mountain or their island, not because they couldn't, but because they were scared they'd miss something.

Nick, who runs the office supply store and is completely reliable, told me today that the people who work for the mammoth computer factory, which is the main employer around here, all die before they hit sixty. Doesn't matter if they eat yogurt or not.

This seems to me to be consistent with Sonia's theory. She died at a ripe old age, by the way.

And I Got This One
for Clapping Erasers

When I was nine years old my parents enrolled me in military school. There are almost no military schools left. Most of them died out during the Vietnam War. But they used to be fairly common. The back pages of classy magazines like *National Geographic* had ads for bunches of them.

These were private boys' schools run along the lines of a little comic-opera army. They dressed the kids up in sissy-looking uniforms and had us march around with rifles.

They were supposed to build character, and give a superior education. The traditional reason for sending a boy to military school was that he was an unmanageable, rotten little predelinquent. I never knew why my parents sent *me*. I always assumed it was because my father came from Europe, and didn't fully understand how things were done here. He had some money at the time, and wanted me educated with the ruling class. My mother liked the uniforms, and thought the students were very polite.

I actually didn't mind the place. School was school, and in the private institution, I got to learn about class snobbery, anti-Semitism, sadism, and the rich variety of sexual practices in which humans indulge. Also, I got to go to class with future corporate raiders, divorce lawyers and plastic surgeons. I had a fairly good time.

The military side of things eluded me pretty much completely. I was no good at keeping my buttons and shoes shiny, my clothes unwrinkled, my hat unlost, my shirt tucked in. I also tended to be late, sloppy, noisy, and a disgrace on the parade ground. My failure as a soldier did not depress me. Since I was socially beyond the pale already, the other cadets never bothered to abuse me for being unmilitary and a hideous, disheveled little monstrosity.

At the end of the year they gave out medals. Medals were given out for various accomplishments, but the one medal that everyone respected, the one that was really hard to get, was the good conduct medal. Out of maybe 400 kids, maybe five would get it.

To get this medal, you had to be perfect for an entire year. One mark against you and you were out of the running. Never late, never sloppy, never caught doing anything against the rules. Also you had to snitch on your friends, because they had an honor code. (Ever wonder about that? Why is it an honor code?) Obviously, by ratting on people you'd make enemies who would try to get you in trouble—and when they realized you were bucking for the good conduct medal, they'd do everything they could to trip you up.

I decided to go for it. The next year, I was a perfect cadet. My buttons shone like mirrors. My shoes too. I was on time for everything. Not only was I sharp on the parade ground—I marched everywhere I went in case anybody was watching. And I turned people in for everything from chewing gum to bestiality. I was a perfect little Nazi. The teachers loved it.

I kept it up for the whole school year. And I got the medal. Beautiful it was, genuine gold-plated, hanging from a red and yellow ribbon. The most unattainable prize the school offered. The commander of the Corps of Cadets didn't have it. The Cadet

Adjutant didn't have it. None of the Cadet Captains had it. I
had it.

And I wore it all the next year. On my filthy, rumpled dirty
dress uniform jacket I wore it. On my everyday uniform blouse,
I wore the little red and yellow ribbon that signified the medal
right over my unbuttoned pocket, the one with the pack of
Luckies in it. My shoes were turning gray and starting to crack.
My buttons were turning green, and my hat was rotting on the
roof of the gym, where I'd thrown it the first day of school. I
cut classes and did a lot of reading for pleasure that year.

The next year I talked my parents into letting me transfer to
public school. I was ready for new worlds to conquer.

Hey Kids, What Time Is It?

I watched the debate between Lloyd Bentsen and Dan Quayle with a lot of pleasure. For some reason it gave me a warm, secure feeling. This puzzled me. Intellectually, it was clear to me that I was watching a fairly embarrassing performance. Two senators, one a smooth, rich, Texan professional politician, and the other, who appeared to be the slowest-thinking mammal on earth, spoke one- and two-minute campaign advertisements.

There was maybe ten minutes of content in the hour and a half. So why did I find it so enjoyable? I even dreamed about it, and woke up feeling peaceful and happy.

It was cozy. It made me feel like a little kid. I remembered family rooms from long ago, dark furniture of a type now seen only in Salvation Army outlets, the smell of carpets made of wool, and the miraculous blue light of the infant television, then a medium with more charm than power.

It reminded me of my favorite show in those days of the seven-inch screen. "Howdy Doody." This was a kid's show with a tall, avuncular host—a westerner, Buffalo Bob, and a irrepressible boy—a puppet, Howdy Doody, a little on the smarmy side, but withal perky and lovable. There was a studio audience, the Peanut Gallery, a bunch of kids who cheered on cue.

And there was a clown, Clarabell, who ran around squirting everyone with seltzer—an element the debate sadly lacked.

It was the characters and their appearance on television that prompted this nostalgia trip. The script did not come up to the "Howdy Doody" show as I remember it. In my imagination, I fixed it up a little bit. Howdy Doody, played by Dan Quayle, has been hypnotized by the evil Mr. Bluster into believing that he's a candidate for vice-president of Doodyville.

Chief Thunderthud, an Indian medicine man, warns Buffalo Bob (Lloyd Bentsen) that it would be dangerous to wake Howdy Doody, or contradict him. So, to humor Howdy, they organize a debate.

As the actual debate fades into history, it blends with my recollections of childhood television, and leaves me with a composite image of a show I can almost believe I saw.

And there's another image that came back to me amongst all these meanderings of memory and association. A schoolmate who used to remind me of Howdy Doody.

This was Klina, B. In the military school, if a kid had a brother in attendance, they'd differentiate by giving them their first initals as last names. So the elder brother was Klina, W., and the kid who looked like Howdy Doody and Dan Quayle was Klina, B.

But while Dan and Howdy are spunky and bright, Klina, B., was wretched, malevolent, and despised. He was like the dark and desperate side of the cheerful mannequin.

Klina, B., was tousled and unkempt. He slouched and slumped. He had dark circles under his eyes. He looked just like the illustration of the chronic masturbator in the hygiene book. Klina, B.'s speech was slow, he seemed confused much of the time, and he frequently fell asleep at his desk.

Looking back, I realize that this was a sorry kid, who probably had awful problems, and needed treatment. At the time, he was simply considered a jerk, and everyone in the fourth grade beat him up, which was easy to do, whenever possible.

Everyone beat him up—except me. I never laid a hand on
Klina, B. I myself, as the son of a commercial Jew, ranked only
a little higher in the pecking order, and had had my share of
unfair fights. Because of that I developed a measure of sympathy
for the poor little slob. It was a matter of secret pride that I
never picked on Klina, B. I felt good about it. I was morally
superior to the rest of the fourth grade.

One day, the teacher said, "Klina, B., and Pinkwater, will
you please go to the book room and bring back twelve copies
of *Modern Arithmetic?*"

We went. The book room was in another building. To go
there, we had to walk through a tree-shaded corridor, which was
the location of choice for fistfights and ambushes. To our right
was the back side of bleachers, which faced the parade ground.
To our left was a building, the windows of which were high
above our heads, and closed. We could not be seen or heard.

When we got to this concealed area, Klina, B., who had not
said a word to me as yet, stopped and faced me. His expression
was resigned—and maybe a little bored. Without warning, he
bashed me right in the nose.

There was nothing else to do, according to my lights at the
time. I pounded the spit out him. I did a good job, but without
enthusiasm. I understood what had motivated him—I just didn't
know any other way to deal with it. He was accustomed to being
beaten to a pulp on that very spot, and was just doing himself
the favor of eliminating the tension of waiting for it.

After I finished massacring him, we went on and got the
textbooks, and carried them back to the classroom without either
of us saying a word.

Klina, B. I wonder what became of the little sad sack.

Polly Wants a Broad-Spectrum Antibiotic

My father used to say, "I yam no back nomberr. I yam a tventiet'-century man." In fact, he was born a few years short of the present century, but he loved everything modern, and detested anything suggestive of the past. Of course, he had curious ideas about what constituted twentieth-century life.

One of his ideas of modernity was to live in a house decorated in light colors with plenty of exotic pets. His taste ran to Chihuahua dogs and monkeys—which animals he never brought home, but constantly threatened to, making me a nervous wreck as a kid. I knew a sissy pet could destroy my reputation in the neighborhood. A shaggy collie or a German shepherd was out of the question—too much of a nineteenth-century quality to dogs like that. He fantasized constantly about iguanas, giant tortoises, lemurs, and cockatoos, but for years we remained petless.

When he finally took the plunge, it was parrots he chose. This was right after World War Two, in Chicago. Very few people had parrots, and there wasn't a whole lot known about their care—or where to get one. My father got one—the first of a number of Psittaciformes we'd own—a double yellow-head Panama named Pedro.

Anyone acquainted with parrots will tell you they're crazy. Intelligent, yes. Affectionate. But also psychotic. Pedro was a self-contained sort of bird who would tear anyone who approached him to shreds—except my father, of course. He loved my father.

After spending a day amusing himself by vocalizing insanely, and tossing sunflower-seed shells in a nine-foot-radius around his perch, Pedro would sense my father's imminent arrival, home from work. Pedro knew when my father was precisely thirty minutes from the front door. At this point he would begin crowing and cooing insistently. This performance would accelerate until he was shrieking and convulsing, flapping and hyperventilating. By the time my father actually came through the door, Pedro would have worked himself into a fit. His feathers awry, his pupils dilating and contracting, he'd be hanging upside down, gripping his perch with one zygodactylous claw.

My father would have to gather Pedro up, and cradle him in his arms, arranging his feathers and comforting him, while Pedro made deranged croaking noises.

Weekends, my father would hang around the house in his underwear. If visitors came, he would put his pants on—if they were friends of his—if not, not. Pedro had the freedom of the house. He would come careening out of the dining room (Pedro was not a good flier) and land on my father, powerful talons wrapped around his clavicle, a trickle of blood appearing on his undershirt. My father would stroke Pedro.

"Dot's a good boid," he would say, "a good boid."

Pedro fell ill. There wasn't a vet in all of Chicago who dealt with parrots. Besides, it was too cold to risk taking him outside. The zoo vet said it sounded like pneumonia. Keep him warm and give him stimulants.

A cruel fate caused the boiler to quit during Pedro's crisis. Everybody moved into the kitchen to keep warm. My father stayed home from work to nurse him. I remember coming home from school upon this scene: Pedro was wrapped in a dishtowel.

To immobilize him, my father had made a sort of cradle out of one of those black enamel oval roasting pans. He had Pedro resting on the open oven door, and was in the act of pouring Ballantine's scotch down Pedro's beak out of a shot glass. Pedro was looking around wildly. What could he have been thinking?

I figure the bird died of fear as much as anything else.

PART FOUR

MAN MEETS DOG

Bootsie

The household pets of my childhood were mostly reflections of my father's eccentricity, and dominance: parrots, lizards, and a miniature Boston bull terrier, Bootsie. Bootsie was terrified of my father, and wet the carpet whenever he spoke to her.

Bootsie made a good deal of noise when sleeping. She had a delicate stomach. My mother had to cook special food for her—hearts and livers—stewed. Prescription dog food was not yet known.

Bootsie was an embarrassment around the neighborhood. This was that period of childhood wherein casual street-life is important. Hanging around with one's bike or one's dog, running into local age-mates, and developing rudimentary social skills were the primary activities. It is to the credit of the other boys on the block that nobody ever said anything disparaging about Bootsie. On the other hand, they didn't have to. It was all too obvious. Already I was an outsized kid, similar to a blimp in shape. A nervous, wheezing little dog, looking like some trained flea at the end of its leash, was all I needed to emphasize my awkwardness.

Occasionally, I would run into a neighborhood dog—an Alaskan husky. If I only had a dog like that, I thought. It was an outdoorsy dog, rough and shaggy and good-humored. The husky

111

simply ignored Bootsie when we'd meet. I myself tried to pretend that I was walking her for someone else.

I may have brought up the possibility of a big collie or even a husky, in conversation with my father. If I did, it no doubt prompted him to begin scouring the classifieds and circling ads for Pomeranians, papillons, teacup poodles and Japanese spaniels. It was wiser not to get him started. His taste in canines, I believe, is a subject for psychiatric evaluation, and not suitable for discussion by a son.

I secretly, disloyally, hated Bootsie. Bootsie reciprocated my feelings, or didn't care to begin with. I know this because she would leave home every chance she got. She'd burrow under the fence—two or three days would pass, and we'd get a call from miles away. Someone would have found Bootsie, and read our phone number off her collar.

My mother didn't drive, and Bootsie would usually come home in the back seat of a taxi. She'd hang around for a couple of weeks, and then run off again. One day she left and never came back. I was not heartbroken.

Bootsie was replaced by the only normal-type animal we ever owned: Nelly, a medium-sized mongrel that came, air freight, from my father's aging brother in Brooklyn.

Uncle Boris had decided that he was too old to keep a dog— or that the dog needed to live in California in a house with a yard—or it may have just been another instance of his lifelong practice of sending unwanted gifts. Sometimes, after the recipient had sent a thank-you note, he'd send a bill.

Nelly was shaggy, flop-eared and two-toned, the sort of dog any boy would want. However, having been raised by a cranky old Jewish man, she instantly attached herself to my father. She pretty much ignored me completely.

This intensified my fantasies about having a really good dog of my own—preferably one on the order of Yukon King, the lead dog of Sergeant Preston, one of my favorite radio adventure characters.

And I did get such a dog. More than one. Years later, I finally became involved with malamute dogs—the only creatures on earth crazier than my own family.

Man Meets Dog

The first time I began to think about getting a dog, as an adult, was when I worked as an art teacher at the Wee Folks Residential Treatment Center in New Jersey. Some of the "wee folks" had to shave every day, and hired out to do farm work in the summer.

I found them somewhat intimidating.

Every day it was a question whether my 2 P.M. class would eat me alive.

"It sure would be nice if I had a big, loyal, scary dog to bring to work with me," I'd think.

Initially, I had fantasized about a tame gorilla, who would obey only me. The ape would crouch under the table mumbling—and my class of 200-pound, muscle-bound sociopaths would take care to remain docile.

As I worked on the concept, I considered that the gorilla was a little bit out of the question, never mind how much fun he'd be at tollbooths. I changed the role to accommodate a timber wolf—and that evolved into a big dog.

Incidentally, there were two or three dogs wandering loose on the grounds—and the day I could bribe and entice one of them to visit the art room would be a day without incident. The kids were not intimidated by the dogs—they felt protective of them. Badly disturbed, acting-out kids would contain themselves

114

rather than upset the pooch. There have been some studies, I believe, of the use of pets in various sorts of treatment—and the results have been dramatic.

I, however, was moving away from the front lines of mental health care and toward a life of literary art and domesticity. I got married and quit my job, in that order.

I left the world of the Wee Folks Residential Treatment Center for the tranquil and idyllic one of the aspiring writer. While my wife knocked herself out, teaching at a university, I had nothing to do but sit by my typewriter and give my fancy free range.

One of the things I liked to think about was getting a dog. I had purchased a bunch of booklets that described various breeds. The texts were virtually identical. Only the pictures were different. I would study the pictures and try to imagine which breed would best enhance my image.

I read a book by Konrad Lorenz, *Man Meets Dog*, a Teutonic fairy tale, but what did I know?

Lorenz puts forward the notion that there are two races of dogs: those descended from jackals and those descended from wolves.

The jackal descendants are fawning, perpetually immature, servile, anxious to please, and any man's best friend.

The wolf-dogs are noble, aloof, serious, dignified. They're one-man dogs, and that man must be a man, my son! To get one of these dogs of northern blood to respect you, you have to have a character as pure and virtuous as theirs—a near-impossibility for all but the most select of humans.

Lorenz suggests that for the ordinary jerk, a mix of the two types—wolf and jackal—is ideal, but the implication is that for heroes there is only one kind of dog: the famous wolf-spitz group, including the Greenland Eskimo dog, the malamute, the husky, and a few others.

This stuff is strictly from Goebbels or the brothers Grimm.

The fact is, all dogs are descended from wolves—that includes Pomeranians, pugs, Great Danes, and jackals.

After he had influenced millions, Lorenz himself recanted. He admitted that he had cooked up the whole theory one night after drinking a lot of kirschwasser and listening to his Wagner records—but by this time, we were living with not one, but two, enormous Alaskan malamutes.

They were nothing like Konrad Lorenz's description of noble northern wolf-dogs. Mostly, they were like the kids I'd taught at the Wee Folks Residential Treatment Center—only maybe with more energy.

The Coming of Juno

We drove into the country on a snowy February day, to pick out a puppy. We had decided on an Alaskan malamute. Actually, getting a malamute was my idea. Jill, who loves all animals, was just going along with it. I had only ever seen two malamutes in the flesh—a brace of beauties that flashed past the car window one night in Manhattan.

For the rest, all I knew about malamutes I had read in books. In particular, one of those little booklets they sell in pet shops. It had excellent color pictures.

Following directions I'd taken over the phone, we traveled a number of country roads, and found Mal-Adroit Kennels. It was a new-looking split ranch, set in the middle of a big field. There was a stand of trees behind the house, and that was where the kennel was. We realized this when, as we began to crunch across the snow at least 40 lupine voices were raised in a howl that caused the hair on the back of my neck to stand up.

If I hadn't been showing off in front of my wife, I would have turned around and driven home right then.

Instead we trudged up to the house and met Larry Porketta. Larry was fatter than me, needed a shave, and was wearing dirty-looking thermal underwear, overalls and insulated boots. I had no basis for comparison at the time, but as dog breeders

117

go, he was better than average. He could read and write, and had never eaten a child of his own.

Larry was a super salesman. Instantly he launched into the technique of flattering me and treating me like an expert. This is sure-fire when dealing with a man and a woman. I knew zilch, less than zip, about dogs—but here was a chance to impress Jill.

Larry Porketta was soliciting my opinion about this and that, peppering me with jargon.

"This one's dam went best of opposite bitch reserve at the Grand National Bahamian Specialty last summer," he'd say— and I would nod gravely.

"Oh, I can see you're a superior judge of dog flesh," Larry said. "Never mind this batch of pups—slunky hocks—but look who I'm telling about slunky hocks. I'll bet you noticed their fettles were undershot before I said a word."

I don't have to tell you, I didn't have any idea what he was talking about. I did sense that he was in complete control—but I wasn't sure what to do about it.

While Larry Porketta was speaking, his wife and daughters were bringing armload after armload of puppies into the small living room. There must have been three dozen pups of all sizes, scampering around, not to mention two or three adult nursing mothers.

Up close the dogs seemed huge. I was a little afraid of them.

Larry Porketta spoke incessantly. He was discussing the virtues and drawbacks of various puppies. Not only did I not understand what he was saying, I didn't know which puppy he was saying it about.

"Now let me explain about breeders' terms," he was saying. "This little lady is Mal-Adroit's Song of Bernadette (my wife's favorite movie). Should you wish to purchase this pup, you have to promise to breed her at least twice, and give me the first and third pick of each litter. Any other pups, I can sell for you on commission, and you'll realize a handsome profit. If you agree to breed her four times, I will waive the stud fee, and pay for all the puppies' shots."

Porketta was trying to involve me in a pyramid scheme. He did with dogs like they do with vitamins and home cleaning products. At one point he was explaining how he could set me up with a complete kennel, and how I could recruit other prospects for the Porketta system.

Meanwhile, Jill was sitting on the floor fooling with the only puppy in the place that looked sick to me. It was slow-moving and listless; its coat was coarse and its eyes were dull. It was coughing. She was cuddling it. I know the woman. In a matter of moments she'd bond with the little sad sack. Then it would be months of medical crises, vet bills and finally agony and death.

I had to act fast. A puppy, larger than any of the others, had just been let in. It bounded around the room, knocking over every other pup. This pup was mostly black with a look of hilarious deviltry in its eyes.

There wasn't any question, this one was healthy.

"I've made up my mind!" I shouted. "I want to buy that puppy!"

"Never!" Larry Porketta responded. "You are pointing at Mal-Adroit's Abishag. That dog I picked out for myself! She has astonishing potential. I expect to achieve fame and greatness with this animal. She's not for sale, and that's final."

"How much?" I asked him.

"Five hundred dollars."

"I'll give you four-fifty and you'll never see me again."

"Done!"

That was how we acquired Mal-Adroit's Abishag, who we never called anything but Juno. Larry Porketta tried to throw in

the sick puppy for an extra fifty bucks, but I outstepped him.
I distracted him with cash, and hustled Jill and Juno out to the
car.

We drove away, ready to begin an important passage in our
lives, which would result in our becoming noted dog trainers,
writing a classic book on the subject, and learning the *truth*
about malamutes.

Life with Juno

The reasons we chose an Alaskan malamute when we decided to get a dog were the beauty of the animals and their reputation. This reputation has it that they are possessed of a kind of dignity and character beyond other dogs that have evolved further from the ancestral wolf. The malamute is seen by some as a sort of noble savage—never fully tame, a link with the wild.

This is true enough, if you consider that the wild is a complicated sort of place, and that wolves are not so much noble and wise as crafty, sneaky, and frequently silly.

Juno was the first malamute I got to know well—and the first dog I'd ever had that was truly my dog. She came to live with us when she was three months old. And almost at once began to initiate us into the tribal secrets of malamute dogs.

This is the lowdown on the noble wolf-dogs of the north: They're hierarchical. In the primitive wolf pack, there is a leader, and there are followers. When you understand this, you understand almost everything.

Every dog has a place in the pecking order, and if it lives with a family, the humans are included, and assigned ranks—by the dog.

Ideally, the leader of the pack is a human. What one doesn't think about until one tries it is that participants in strict hierarchies tend to be upwardly mobile. The dog might acknowledge you as leader—but there needn't be anything permanent about it. You might die or go blind.

In our family dog-pack, I got to be the leader. I thought this was as it should be. I didn't know then that all dogs automatically love and obey Jill—and she got Juno to imprint on me by ignoring her, shoving her away, and giving her sneaky punches when Juno was small.

So it was me as Lord Wolf. Jill was second in authority, Juno was third, and the cat came in fourth. Juno set about trying to erode Jill's authority, so she, Juno, could move up to second place. There was nothing fierce or overtly nasty about this— she would just do things to Jill, like tripping her, ripping her clothes, and constantly scheming to wriggle into bed, under the covers, and wind up in Jill's place, with her head on Jill's pillow.

Me, her master, she tested periodically to see whether I might have lost any of my wolfish authority. She did this by playfully bowling me over, ignoring specific commands, and peeing on the floor while looking me in the eye.

Juno was trainable—but she wasn't going to make it easy for us. Not everyone would have found Juno's antics funny—but the truth is, we did. Jill and I had both had had plenty of jobs working with disturbed and delinquent kids, and we appreciated a challenge.

There were two categories of circumstance under which Juno quit being a clown—major snowstorms, and on wilderness trails.

When there was heavy snow, Juno became very businesslike. She'd switch into four-wheel drive and turn on her radar. Juno appeared to be able to locate things under snow, and to find landmarks that had been transformed by snow as if there weren't any snow at all. She would also watch snow in a way that suggested that she was getting a lot more information than I could.

On hikes, Juno would insist I return exactly the way I had come. If there were a big rock, for example, and I had gone around the east side of it, Juno would physically force me to go around it the same way on the return trip. If I took her back along the same trail a year later, she'd remember the rock, and steer me around it identically. As far as I could tell, she never forgot anything she'd seen by way of topography, and generally knew where she was at all times.

She also was able to carry her own food in a special doggie-rucksack, and could not get tired. If we met anyone on the trail, she was friendly. Nights, if anyone or anything came into camp, she'd scare the hell out of them.

The one single moment that comes closest to summing up my friendship with Juno—and the whole reason for liking dogs—took place not far from my home at the time, on those cliffs on the west side of the Hudson River. Juno and I had been hiking strenuously, and we were taking a rest. We were sitting on a rock, looking out over the river, toward Westchester County. It was a perfect spring day, gold and blue and green. We felt good.

After a while, I began to realize that the dog and I were sharing a thought. It wasn't anything very special or complicated—it was something a man could think, and a dog could think. It was just something like . . . "Ahh!"

Arnold!

elling us Arnold, our second Alaskan malamute, was Larry
Porketta's masterpiece. Only selling a dog already dead,
or made of acrylic, would have been more of a coup.

"This pup is special," Larry said.

"He looks sort of scuzzy," I said.

"He's six months old. It's an awkward age for malamutes.
That's why I'm prepared to let him go for a pittance."

"He's sort of runty and scrawny, isn't he?"

"Not at all. In fact, he's big for his size. Here, feel of him."

He thrust the puppy into my arms. It licked my face. Jill
reached over to hug the puppy, and got kissed too.

We were goners. We took Arnold with us.

When we got him home and looked at him in a good light,
we could see that his head was too big for his body, his tail
appeared to be screwed on wrong, and he had a tendency to
bump into things.

There was nothing right with Arnold! Half his weight was
intestinal worms. He had a bad cough. His feet stank, and he
would have a fit if he heard a sudden noise.

In time, Arnold calmed down a bit. He didn't hit the ceiling
whenever a truck rolled by. He grew into proportion, and got
to be downright handsome. He also began to exhibit a sort of
charm and . . . well . . . suavity and elegance.

124

But he also began to show a side we never dreamed he had. He turned into fighter. He didn't fight with Juno, our first malamute. She had wisely begun to intimidate him from the first day—and he never lost his respect for her quick tooth.

Arnold's potential opponents—actually his victims—were all dogs on earth, other than Juno.

Our best guess is that during the six months Arnold had lived before we got him he'd been abused in various ways by humans and dogs. Now he was evening the score.

Malamutes were bred to pull freight. It's not unheard of for them to move a ton in weight-pulling contests. If Arnold saw a German shepherd he wanted to destroy while being walked on a leash, it took some doing to keep it from happening.

We must have read a hundred books about dog training.

I consulted numerous experts. Some of these people were remarkable. They had brilliant theories about how Arnold got to be so antisocial. None of them had any useful suggestions about how to turn him around.

One trainer suggested a method. First, we'd have to find another aggressive malamute, whose owner wanted to cure him. Then we'd muzzle the two of them so they couldn't harm one another, tie them together by the collar with a cord two feet long, and throw them into a closet for an hour or so. This way they'd get it out of their system, the trainer explained. They'd try to fight, get frustrated, fall asleep, wake up, try again, and so forth, until they were sick of the whole business.

We tried it.

All that happend was that Arnold learned how to menace another dog while taking a nap. When I peeked into the closet, Arnold was fast asleep, growling loudly, and the other malamute was crying for its mother.

Next we simply enrolled Arnold in an ordinary dog obedience class—the kind they have at the local VFW or adult ed program.

We warned the instructor, of course, and Arnold wore his muzzle to class.

These classes are usually held in some gymnasium or similar space—and they're a little like a square dance. The instructor stands in the middle of the room, calling out commands, and the trainees and dogs march around, doing his bidding.

At first I simply dragged Arnold around the floor. He'd travel on his back or side much of the time, pawing the air and screaming threats at the other dogs. Occasionally, he'd grovel and paw his way toward some terrified poodle—and I'd drag him away.

Each course lasted six or eight weeks. Arnold went through six courses—all identical, all beginners' obedience. By the third course, I was able to dispense with the muzzle.

Arnold continued vocalizing, but I had become so strong and expert in handling the leash that I could control his occasional lunges at some innocent beagle.

Juno, mostly from just watching, week after week, had become a sort of obedience genius, and we'd take her out and win trophies with her on weekends.

A full two years after I'd started trying to train Arnold, I took him to an obedience match sponsored by the local malamute club. It was an all-northern dog match—Siberian huskies, malamutes, Samoyeds and Akitas—all of them feisty and scrappy by nature. The match was held indoors—space was limited— and Arnold brushed up against a number of tough customers.

Arnold never raised a lip to any of them—even though he had several explicit invitations. When it was his turn to compete, he turned in a record low score. People must have thought I was crazy, beaming with pride as I was.

On the way home, I bought Arnold his very own Big Mac and a milk shake—as I had promised I'd do if he kept his choppers off the other dogs at the match.

It was possible to live with Arnold after that. He was never perfect, but he had some remarkable qualities. I wouldn't want to go through the experience of training a crazy animal again, but I'm glad I did it once. He taught me a lot, that dog.

The Soul of a Dog

Once, Jill had fun with our Alaskan malamute, Arnold, by pretending that she was teaching him a nursery song. It was pure nonsense—Jill was tending our old-fashioned, non-automatic clothes washer, and Arnold was keeping her company.

Jill sang him the song about the eensy beensy spider, and indicated where he was supposed to join in. He did so, with something between a scream of anguish and the call of a moose in rut.

The next time she had laundry to do, Arnold appeared, and sat squirming excitedly until she sang him the song. He came in on cue. Arnold learned a number of songs. His vocal range was limited, but his ear was good.

It was also Arnold who taught Juno, our other dog, to set up a howl whenever we passed a McDonald's. On a vacation trip, we'd breakfasted on Egg McMuffins for a week, and the dogs always got an English muffin. They never forgot.

I once observed Arnold taking care of an eight-week-old kitten. The kitten was in a cage. Arnold wanted to go and sleep in his private corner, but every time the kitten cried, he'd drag himself to his feet, slouch over to the cage and lie down with his nose between the wires, so the kitten could sink its tiny claws into it. When the kitten became quiet, Arnold would head for his corner and flop, exhausted. Immediately the kitten would cry, and Arnold would haul himself back to the cage. I counted this performance repeated over forty times.

Arnold acquired friends. People would visit him.

My friend Don Yee would borrow Arnold sometimes, and they'd drive to the White Castle and eat hamburgers.

He was the sort of dog you could talk things over with.

But he was not just a good listener, affable eccentric and bon vivant. He was a magnificent athlete. While Juno was tireless and efficient on the trail, Arnold made locomotion an art—a ballet.

Watching Arnold run flat-out in a large open space was unforgettable, and opened a window to something exceedingly ancient and precious—a link to the first time men followed dogs, and hunted to live.

He was a splendid companion—and he would pull you up a steep hill, if you were tired.

In a way, the hardest thing about living with dogs in modern times is related to the excellent care we give them.

Vast sums are spent by pet food companies devising beautifully balanced, cheap, palatable diets. Vet care these days is superb—and most pet owners take advantage of it.

As a result, dogs live longer than they may have done, and survive illnesses that they would not have survived in earlier times. And it very often falls to us to decide when a dog's life has to end—when suffering has come to outweigh satisfaction.

When it came Arnold's time to die, it was I who decided it. I called the vet and told him I was bringing Arnold in.

He knew about malamute vigor. He prepared a syringe with twice the dose it would take to put a dog Arnold's size to sleep. "Put to sleep" is an apt euphemism. It's simply an overdose of a sleeping drug. The dog feels nothing.

"There's enough in here for a gorilla," the vet wisecracked weakly. He was uncomfortable with what he had to do.

Arnold, of course, was completely comfortable—doing his best to put everyone else at ease.

I held Arnold while the vet tied off a vein.

"This will take six, maybe eight seconds at most," the vet said. He injected the fluid.

Nothing happened. Arnold, who had been completely relaxed, was now somewhat intent—but not unconscious, not dead.

"Sometimes it takes a little longer," the vet said. It had been a full half minute. Arnold was looking around.

The vet was perspiring—getting panicky. I knew what he was thinking. Some ghastly error. The wrong stuff in the syringe. More than a minute had passed.

A crazy thought occurred to me. Was it possible? Was Arnold waiting for me to give him leave to go? I rubbed his shoulders and spoke to him. "It's OK, Arnold. I release you." Instantly he died.

I swear I felt his spirit leave his body.

The vet and I went outside and cried for a quarter of an hour.

He was an awfully good dog.

Arnold Comes Home

I thought I saw Arnold today," Jill told me. Jill's thought that the dog she had seen might have been Arnold, our Alaskan malamute, was momentary, until she remembered that he'd been dead for a year and a half.

It was a dog running loose in the neighborhood that looked exactly like Arnold. Jill had jammed on the brakes, and spoken to a neighbor. Did he know that dog? He did. It was always hanging around with his dog.

This was the neighbor who had been working for a solid year underneath the truck with "Colorado or Bust" painted on the side—not an ideal person to ask about anything, but it was a simple question.

Jill went about her business, marveling at the resemblance, and muttering about people who let their dogs run loose. That night she told me about the incident.

We were living in an ordinary suburban neighborhood of one-family houses with little backyards. A few minutes away, near the railroad station, was all that was left of the last dairy farm in town. There, in a pasture full of nettles, rented from the retired dairy farmer, Jill kept a couple of horses.

When we moved from Hoboken to the suburbs, we went in to the hilt.

Jill would drive over to the farm three or four times a day to tend the horses. The day after she had sighted the dog that looked like Arnold, she took off as usual, early in the morning, for the farm. I kept sleeping.

I was awakened by the telephone. It was Jill, calling from the deli across the street from the farm. "You'd better get over here," she said. "Something you have to see."

I jumped into our second car—I told you we had hit suburban life heavily—and drove down to the farm . . . where I found . . . well, it was Arnold . . . sitting in the back seat of Jill's car. Arnold—or whoever this was—gave me a friendly kiss on the face when I looked into the car. This dog was a female— but otherwise a ringer in appearance and attitude.

Arnold had a couple of characteristic postures in automobiles. One was sitting facing backward in the back seat. Another was sitting with his haunches on the seat and his forepaws on the floor. This dog assumed both positions while I watched.

"Spooky, isn't it?" Jill said.

It seems when Jill had arrived at the farm, this dog—this Arnold clone—was lying dead in the driveway. It had obviously been run over, and had staggered this far and expired. A small crowd had gathered and were feeling sorry for the poor dead dog, and discussing what to do with the carcass.

Jill yanked the emergency and went over and knelt by the body. She lifted a paw, which dropped limply, but not deadly, she thought. Then she thought she noticed a tiny twitching around the eye.

Malamutes, some of them, can sleep like nothing else that's animate. Convinced that there is nothing on earth that wants to hurt them, they can drop off in the middle of noise and crowds and sleep like cinder blocks.

Jill gave the whistle she'd used to give Arnold, and the dead dog sprang to its feet and jumped into her car. Jill got a container of coffee from the deli, thought it over for a while, and phoned me.

We took the dog to the neighbor—the one with the truck. On closer inspection, he allowed that he'd never seen this dog before. There were no tags, of course.

We took the dog home. She trotted right to the front door. Juno, the other malamute, and the housecats gave a sniff, and went about their business. "No big deal," they seemed to say. "Arnold's back, that's all."

We called the various pounds and shelters, read the classifieds, and placed an ad of our own in the paper.

Nobody claimed her. She's with us still, nine years later. We named her Arctic Flake. She doesn't remind me of Arnold as much as she used to. She's got qualities of her own, different from his.

Of course, we've worked up any number of theories about what happened, and how Flake came to us. We're not sure what we believe. For those who are interested, Flakey turned up just a year and a half after Arnold died, and the vet said that, as nearly as he could tell, she was just a year and half old.

Jacques

All the stories I've told so far have taken place in the past—ten to almost twenty years ago.

Since then, we've always had dogs around. Arctic Flake is still with us, of course—Jill says we have to have at least one malamute; she doesn't feel normal without one. But I hadn't done any training to speak of—not even with our own dogs; none of them seem to really enjoy it—until lately.

Every so often I take a walk through the local pound. It's a holdover from the old days. I study the different types—size up the available talent. Sometimes I find a dog with that special quality, and my Jill and I try to help find it a home. We offer to give training tips to whoever will adopt it, and donate a book on dog care to make a more appealing package.

Recently, I came across a three-year-old mongrel—shepherd and something northern. There was something about his expression—his eyes—the way he approached me. It was Arnold again—and Flakey. I've got a half-baked idea that dogs have a finite, limited and comparatively small number of souls, which they share. According to my theory—if you can call it that—it is possible to meet the same dog over and over again—and one does.

I went home and got Jill. She doesn't like visiting the pound. She says it's like being a tourist in a concentration camp. The dogs that don't get adopted die—and they know it. I insisted she come see him. I wanted to know if she saw what I saw.

She did. "You going to take him home?" she asked me.

"No," I said. "We've got three dogs. We're full up. We'll just offer the book, and the free advice."

"You can take him if you want him," Jill said.

"No. I just wanted you to see him. He'll get a home."

"What if he doesn't?"

"He will."

Jill understood something I didn't about my periodic trips to the pound. She knew I was looking for a dog of my own. I haven't had a personal dog in years. One of the house dogs, a black chow chow named Bear, looks upon himself as my dog—but he also appears to be a student of Zen, or some other esoteric practice based on nonattachment. His mode of showing affection is to visit me in my office once or twice a week, and fall asleep. He has bad hips, so he can't go for long walks. I take him for car rides. It's a low-intensity relationship.

I don't have to tell you that the shepherd/Akita cross came home with Jill when his week was up and he hadn't been adopted.

I've been getting up early for the past two weeks to train Jacques.

The way I train dogs is pretty standard. The process is incremental. First you teach the dog to sit. "Sit!" you say, and help him do it. When he gets it wrong, you say, "No!" Then "Sit!" again, and when he does it, you tell him, "Good dog!"

This way, he's learning what "sit" means, what "no" means, and how nice it is to be told "good dog." Next you teach him "heel," which means to walk with you at your left side, and "sit" automatically when you stop.

The thing that's remarkable about Jacques is that he appears to be able to anticipate, and put together the elements of his new vocabulary in new ways. For example, he learned to stay put on command when sitting, or lying down. The next day, without any preparation or practice, he caught on that, while walking by my side, he is meant to stop in his tracks when I tell him "stay," while I keep walking without him to the end of the leash.

He's a genius. In two weeks we've already finished what would ordinarily be eight or ten weeks of basic obedience. I've worked with superintelligent dogs, but they've always belonged to someone else. Jacques, I get to keep.

It's not just a matter of his quickly learning the assortment of commands that make him easy to live with and handle—it's what's happening to the two of us. Jacques and I are developing a common language. For my part, I've taught him to understand those few words of English. For his part, he's taught me that when he catches my hand in his mouth and squeezes it gently, it means he loves me.

Train Your Dog, Dammit!

Stop the music, please.

This is not a story. It's an advertisement for dog training.

In telling dog stories, day after day, I believe I've given the impression that when one has a dog, what one does with it is train it.

That's true—but I can imagine reasonable people asking, "Why spend weeks training a dog? I just want one to enjoy."

That's why you should train it—because we all, unless we're sheep ranchers, keep dogs for pleasure. My point is that you can't really enjoy a dog unless you train it.

The most fundamental training every dog that lives indoors receives is housebreaking. It's essential, so people usually find a way to muddle through it—or get rid of the dog. Biting and chewing is another problem most people deal with. You can't have the pup munching on you and your property—so you find a way to make sure he doesn't.

For a lot of people, that's where it stops. And, in fact, you can actually get by with that little bit of training.

I would add not pulling on the leash. Every morning, when I work with Jacques in the park, I see people having their arm pulled out of the socket while they "walk the dog."

Imagine a dog that's just a little more sophisticated than one

137

whose accomplishments are limited to not soiling the house, gnawing on your person, or dragging you down the street.

Imagine a dog that will shut up when you tell it to, go lie down and quit bugging you when you tell it to, sit quietly in the car, behave at the vet's—a dog you can safely leave at home with your furniture, and one that is welcome when you go visiting.

Does that sound like a dog that might give more pleasure than the basic uneducated family hound?

And consider it from the dog's point of view. The main thing any dog wants is to be with you, and participate as much as possible in what you're doing. A trained dog can go more places and be involved in more activities. Plus, the training itself is something the dog gets to do with you—its favorite person.

Have I convinced you? I think so.

Now—how to go about it? There are plenty of training books. None of them are very useful for a beginner. There's a bit of a knack involved—like riding a bicycle. If you'd never ridden a bike, trying to learn how from a manual, while possible, would be terribly difficult. Whereas if you have someone to show you how, it's fairly easy.

So who's going to show you how? Well, you can fly me to wherever you live, house and feed me for a month or so, and pay me a handsome wage. I'll be happy to get you started.

Or, you might decide to go another route—the local dog obedience class sponsored by kennel clubs and such. They take place all over the country in church halls, adult education centers, parks—they're easy to find. It's likely your vet will be able to direct you to one. Most of the courses meet for an hour or so, once a week, and go on for six to ten weeks. The average cost is about thirty-five dollars.

There will be someone there who will show you what to do— and all you need to do besides show up is practice with your dog for fifteen or twenty minutes a day. If you can't spare that much time, a dog is the wrong pet for you.

Sometimes a "puppy kindergarten," early conditioning for very young pups, is offered. I recommend this. In the regular obedience classes, there's a minimum age, which varies.

Just one tip about obedience classes: do not get discouraged and drop out in the first or second week. There is nothing as noisy, confusing and insane as the first night of an obedience class. People and dogs milling about, barking, feeling awkward—it's pure chaos. Some instructors wisely have the people come without their dogs the first week. It's still chaos, but the dogs are spared embarrassment. By the second or third week, it will all start to make sense to you—and your dog.

I've been to a lot of these classes, and I've taught a lot of them. Everybody has a good time, and dogs and owners get healthful exercise. I urge everybody to consider it.

By the way, it doesn't have to be a brand-new puppy you take to school. The old saw about old dogs and new tricks only applies to certain people.

Do You Hear Anything
from Krazy Kat?

Someone told me about an animal psychic. You call her, and over the telephone she will commune with your pets. You send her twenty dollars only if you're satisfied.

Psychics of any sort aren't high on my list of interests, but I was recuperating from surgery, and I was bored and ready for some nonstrenuous diversion. I called the psychic.

She sounded pleasant, moderately well educated, not spooky. She asked me to tell her a little about the animals she was to get in touch with.

I'm no dope. I once spent a couple of days observing and being instructed by a carnival fortune-teller. I know some of the tricks. The main one is to feed back to the customer all the information he's just given you, and add a few educated guesses. Given that most people don't listen to or remember what they say, and are inclined to believe things told them in a sincere tone of voice, even if only ten percent of the guesses are right, it makes a convincing performance.

So I tried to tell the animal psychic lady as little as possible. But she insisted on a few basic facts about my dogs.

She painted a pretty fair picture of the dogs' personalities— but as a former professional dog trainer, I could have done that myself from the descriptions I'd given her. I give her credit for being acquainted with a variety of canine personality types, but I wasn't all that impressed.

We moved on to horses. There are three horses on this place, and I told her their breed, ages and gender—that's all. This time she didn't pump me for more information. Instead she said, "There's something funny here. Didn't you tell me you had an old gelding, a young mare, and a two-year-old filly?"

"That's right."

"Well, I'm talking to an old mare—a fourth horse—and a very unusual horse she is."

There is a fourth horse on our property, but she's underground—deceased. It's our beloved old Icelandic mare, Derry— one of those animals you meet once in a lifetime, with a personality more vivid than most people's.

"This mare is really funny," the psychic said. "She won't let me talk to the other horses. Says if there's anything I want to know, I can ask her—and what am I doing here anyway? You know this horse?"

"Maybe," I said.

"Is this the mother of your seven-year-old?"

"What else is she saying?"

"She says she has everything under control—that she takes care of the other horses, and the humans as well."

"Yep. That's her."

"She says that if anything needs doing, she just stares at your house until your wife comes and deals with it."

"Sounds familiar."

"She says she tells you when to do something to the feet of her daughter—bathe them or something."

Derry's daughter, Pferdel, had a grave case of laminitis, and my wife had amazed the vets by nursing her through it to what looks like a nearly complete recovery—a one-in-ten shot, maybe less. I hadn't mentioned this to the psychic.

"Yes, there has been some trouble with her feet."

"Well, she's a funny old horse. Says she watches over you."

I sent the psychic her twenty dollars. I'm not sure whether she was talking to Derry, or reading my mind.

Of course, fortune-tellers never tell you anything you didn't know already. We'd had the feeling that Derry's been looking after us all along.

PART FIVE

IGUANA BE ALONE

And Zen I Wrote

I'm a pretty good writer. I don't know what you think, but I
think I am, and apparently enough people think so that I've
been able to pay the mortgage all these years. Well, I'm not
going to argue. For the purposes of what I'm going to tell you
about, you will have to assume that I'm a pretty good writer.

I'm better than pretty good, but I don't see why I have to twist
anybody's arm.

This is about how to prepare to be a good writer—or any kind
of artist. It's the kind of information you won't get anywhere
else.

When I was a student I invented a number of practices that,
I vaguely hoped, would help me become a good artist. They are
my own discoveries. I share them with you now, free and for
nothing.

The first thing I did was teach myself to sit at a table. Seems
simple, but not many people can do it. Specifically, I had a lot
of trouble "getting started." People who want to do art use that
phrase a lot. "I can't seem to get started."

Well, I had trouble getting started. So I invented this regimen.
I made a goal of sitting for one hour at the table where I was
supposed to do my work. The rules were, once I sat down, I
was not to get up for one hour. I wasn't obliged to do any work—
but I wasn't allowed to do anything else. It took me a few days

145

to get so that I could sit quietly for a whole hour. If I did manage to sit for an hour—I allowed myself to regard it as my day's successful creative work, even if I hadn't picked up a pencil. When I was able to do an hour, I upped the time to two hours. When I got so that I could sit still for two hours, I invariably started working while sitting. I finally got it so I could sit at the table working, with planned breaks for stretches and the bathroom—I'm not a fanatic nut—for eight continuous hours. That's a long haul for this kind of thing, as any writer or painter will tell you.

The next thing I wanted to do was develop my powers of observation—not my powers of description; that's easier. I wanted to get beyond what I could describe and find strata of experience that I was probably missing. I did two things. The first was to watch the sun set every day for a year. I'm speaking of an academic year, September to June. (I was at college when I did this.) Every day, I went to a place overlooking the Hudson River, and watched the whole sunset. I didn't try to make anything of it, come to any conclusions. I just sat and watched. I believe it did me a lot of good.

Another year I picked a different tree every evening, just before dusk, and watched it until it became dark. Same as the sunsets. I didn't try to draw it or describe it—I just paid attention to it. I can still remember specific trees and sunsets from that time.

At an absolute miniumum, I now have an appreciation of how trees and sunsets look. While I can't prove it, I think I have a better appreciation of how many things look.

The other problem I wanted to address was how to make things in a sustained, spontaneous and unhesitating way. I did this by setting myself a quota of making one woodcut print every day —in addition to anything else I might do. I was obliged to make a drawing on a piece of board, carve it out, roll ink on it, and

make two decent-looking prints from it sometime before going
to sleep. It didn't have to be woodcuts. It could have been poems,
or radio talks.

This wasn't all I did. I did conventional things, took classes,
read stuff, listened to advice. Some of it was useful, some was
not.

And it still took me a while to get to be a swell writer—but
those exercises I just told you about were the most useful things
I did. Fun too. It puts me in a good mood just thinking about
them.

What Has Two Legs and
Chases Katz?

Iused to know a fellow by the name of Lance Gonzales. Lance was a painter. Nights he was a bouncer in a saloon. He seemed to be a pretty bad painter. He was sort of a joke in the neighborhood. Then he got this cat. It walked in through the window one day.

When Lance finished a painting, he'd lean it against the wall, and have a look at it. The cat would do one of two things. He'd go behind the painting, curl up and go to sleep, in which case, Lance would paint over it and try again. Or the cat would fly at the painting and try to claw it to bits. In that case, Lance would lock it in the closet until he could send it off to a juried competition. Every painting the cat hated won a prize.

Also, the cat would try to attack especially good paintings while Lance Gonzales was working on them. Lance got a toy gun that shot a puff of air at a target made of plastic ribbons. It was harmless. He'd wear the gun in his belt while he painted. When he sensed the cat was behind him, he'd spin around and chase the cat away with a blast of air. He said the tension between him and the cat caused the paintings to come out as well as they did. That year, Lance won every major award in the country.

When the cat left, through the same window, Lance's painting ceased to be interesting—and he won no more prizes.

I have a cat. Charles. He's a Manx (no tail). We got him at the local pound.

Charles is mostly blind in one eye. When he was X-rayed the time he got into the road and was run over, we learned that he's got some buckshot in him. Charles has been through a lot.

When Charles moved into the house, he appointed himself my office cat, helper and adviser. For about seven years, he's had the job. When I head for my office, he comes running, and gets there before I do. He works the same hours as me. When I am away from home, he sits outside my office door and makes aggravating noises.

Of late he has taken to hovering behind my chair. The first time I lean forward, he leaps up and wedges himself between the chair back and my back. It takes some doing to pry him loose, and if I do, he'll be back in a minute. If I'm concentrating on something, I tend to forget he's there until my back starts to ache from leaning forward for hours. Sometimes I sadistically lean back and squash him. He likes it. I always lose my nerve and quit squashing before he complains.

He's there as I write this. Or maybe he's not. The small of my back is permanently numb. I imagine I've got a Charles-shaped depression there. I've gotten so I never lean back in my chair. I'm getting stoop-shouldered. I'd ban the little swine from the office, but I'm not sure that his constant presence isn't the secret of my sprightly style.

Nigra Sum sed Formosa

> In Xanadu did Kubla Khan
> A stately pleasure dome decree:
> Where Alph, the sacred river, ran
> Through caverns measureless to man
> Down to a sunless sea.
> [Sound effect: *KNOCK KNOCK*]

"Hey Coleridge, you in there?"

"Wha? Wha? Who izzit? Wha?"

Back when I was trying to be an artist, I used to patronize a dealer in art supplies. His name was Herman Hermann. He operated out of a loft in Manhattan. A lot of artists would deal with no one else, even though he was strangely helpful and destructive in equal measure.

This is a typical incident:

One time, a fellow came in—a painter—wanted to buy some pastel chalks.

"You're in luck," Herman Hermann said. "This is not just some shop! This is Herman Hermann, Fine Art Supplies! These are not merely pastels. These chalks are made in a tiny village in Cornwall. One family makes them—has for generations. Practically their whole yearly output is bought up by Marc Chagall. I happen to have one box."

150

The painter buys the chalks. Then he wants paper.

"In a remote village in Pakistan is a tribe of Oriental Jews who have lived in one place for over three thousand years. They make a paper, once used for sacred documents by the priests of Isis and Osiris. Nobody knows the formula. This paper happens to be perfect for pastel drawing. I guarantee it will last for centuries, and the texture is incredible. Here, feel! Is that paper?"

So the painter lays out six bucks for a single sheet of paper—he's a little confused—he goes home.

Five o'clock the same day, he's back. Herman Hermann is just about to close the shop.

"That stuff you sold me this morning," the painter says.

"Yes?"

"It was everything you said it was! I went home and worked all day on a drawing. The quality of those chalks! The colors, and the feel of them! As if they had a life of their own! And the paper! I never experienced anything like it! And the drawing . . . well, I'm really excited about it. I mean, I'm satisfied. I mean, it's the best thing I've ever done."

"What did I tell you?" Herman Hermann said. "Herman Hermann *knows*."

"Now what I want," the painter said, "is some of that spray fixative. I don't want anything to happen to my drawing."

"Spray fixitive—ptui!" Herman Hermann said. "That stuff is diabolical. Instantly you spray it on, the chemicals start to consume the paper. In twenty years, it's gone. Of course, if you don't use anything, the drawing might get smudged. What are you to do?"

"What?" asked the painter.

"Herman Hermann has the answer," Herman Hermann said. "In Ohio lives an Amish farmer, a genius chemist. In the winter, when there's nothing to do, he makes a fixative in his kitchen. All natural ingredients. You can drink this stuff. It won't hurt you, it won't hurt your drawing. He takes it to a paint factory, and they load it into aerosol cans—with compressed air, no fluorocarbons."

Now the painter is hurrying along the street, shaking up his can of Amish spray fixative. He gets back to his apartment, just as the last rays of the sun are falling on his masterpiece.

He doesn't even take his coat off. He wants to protect his picture. He presses the button, and, of course, out comes a cloud of flat black. Rustoleum. Some mix-up at the paint cannery in Amish country.

It's often like that. Look at that guy pounding on Coleridge's door in the middle of the poem. And just a couple of days ago, I finally wrote something great. I mean, *really* great. It all happened so fast I hardly had time to realize what I had done when something made the computer decide it was no longer going to take orders from humans. The screen froze. I could see a corner of my creation—but the machine would not let go of it. It would not let it be recorded on paper or disk.

I tried to scrawl the piece by hand. Ordinarily, anytime you rewrite something it gets a little better—but this had been perfect! There was only one way for it to go—a few little steps toward mediocrity.

I think the reason those painters were loyal to Herman Hermann was that it was easier to take when it seemed to come from him rather than admit the gods are jealous and destructive.

Iguana Be Alone

There used to be full-page ads in the back of comic books. They were in blindingly tiny type, and offered all sorts of things I wanted. There was trick soap (the more you wash, the dirtier you get), a device for throwing your voice, brass knuckles, X-ray eyeglasses. All good stuff.

The big item, shown across the top of the page, was the pet chameleon. Fifty cents. They could change color. You could wear them attached to your lapel with a tiny leash and collar (twenty-five cents). Amusing and educational pets, the copy read.

I ordered a brace of the things, and a box of special chameleon food. This was the first time I'd ever bought anything through the mail. It was possibly the first time I'd spent as much as a dollar on a purchase. I laboriously penciled my name and address on the order form, stuffed assorted coins into an envelope and mailed it off.

A couple of weeks later, a box came in the mail. It had holes punched in it. I pried off the top. Inside were two brown desiccated-looking things. Incredibly spindly and fragile-looking. Horrible. Were they dead? They didn't look like the drawing in the ad.

These were not true chameleons, I now know, but green anoles (*Anolis caroliniensis*), a common lizard in the southeastern states.

I also did not know then but was rapidly finding out that while not actually phobic, I am uneasy in the presence of reptiles. I am able to admire them at a moderate distance, I can tolerate them when I meet them in the wild, but on an interpersonal level I find reptiles, little tiny feathery hands down, the least attractive things on earth.

These two reptiles, warmed at room temperature, stopped being dead, and flew to the ceiling, where they stuck. I suppose they more or less scampered or jumped, but I remember them flying.

I do not like weightless animals. I fled. I left it to my older sister to collect and deal with the chameleons. She made them a present to Henry, the criminally insane boy downstairs, who tested the lizards' resistance to various kinds of trauma. The lizards did not survive.

I survived, and as a grown man was writing a book in which intelligent lizards figure. This was no doubt some part of an internal healing process, harking back to my childhood experience. The lizards in my book were not wraithlike and nauseating. They stood five feet tall, and spoke English. I quite liked them.

I did not like my publisher. I always have trouble with publishers. Editors in particular annoy me. They're often cold-blooded, tiny-minded, insect-eating, scaly little monsters.

The editor of my lizard book had managed to aggravate me to the point of my quitting work on the book. I was fed up. Besides, I had a lucrative business at the time—I was a dog trainer in Hoboken, New Jersey. I decided not to finish the book, and to tend to other things.

I was sweeping up the puppy school one day, shortly after deciding to down tools on the book, and what should I find, squatting in the middle of the floor? A lizard.

I popped it into a jar, punched holes in the lid, and studied it. It was one of those anoles. Not native to northern New Jersey. At least this one was a healthy green color. Otherwise it could have been one of the pair that had terrified me as a child.

Where had it come from? I tried various theories, and sought the opinions of friends—no good explanation was forthcoming. I gave the lizard to a passing kid. He seemed happy to get it.

A week or so went by, and I had almost forgotten about the lizard, when another one appeared. This one was a bit larger then the first one. It seemed more confident, more self-assured.

This time, I decided, I was going to keep the thing—come to terms with it. I went to the pet shop and got an aquarium, a box of lizard food, put gravel in the aquarium, a tiny water dish, a book on lizard care, a plant. The lizard ignored all these amenities, and just stared at me. He watched me continuously, moving only to get a better view of me as I went about my work.

It didn't take long to get on my nerves. I sent the lizard and all his gear to live in a science class in an elementary school. And I resumed writing the book.

To this day, I don't know where those lizards came from, or what, if anything, this all means. It may be that there in that puppy school in Hoboken, New Jersey, it became my destiny to be a poor writer instead of a rich dog trainer. It may be that there are lizards watching all of us, making sure we stick to our assigned tasks. All I know is that I never saw another one— and I've never quit writing.

Nerds of a Feather

After I graduated from college, I moved to New York, and discovered that everybody I had been friends with in college had done the same thing. I spent my time hanging out with the same people I had hung out with right along.

I liked my friends well enough, but I had gotten fairly bored after four years. Besides, I wanted to get in with a powerful crowd. I wanted to make my mark in the Art World. I wanted to move in new and bigger circles. So I told my buddies that I would appreciate it if they left me alone for a year or so.

"Good idea," they said. "We were getting pretty sick of you too."

Nobody visited me. Days passed during which I didn't speak a word to anybody. As a consequence of which I got terribly lonely. I couldn't very well look up my friends after telling them, in effect, that they weren't interesting or well connected enough for me to waste my time on. I'd made my bed as an ambitious creep.

One day I saw an interesting girl in a shop. We began to converse. Then I blurted out my whole predicament.

"I don't know a soul in New York," I said, "except those people I've chosen to avoid. I want to meet new people, see new things, start a life."

"You're in luck," the girl said. "I happen to be connected

156

with the most advanced and interesting bunch in town. My friends are the hippest, smartest, most creative, most happening people there are. You stick around. In a little while, they're coming for me, and we're all going out for the evening. You come too."

First-rate. Her friends showed up. She introduced me to them, and explained that I wanted to upgrade my social connections. They all said the same thing she'd said. "Daniel Pinkwater, you are a lucky man. We know the best spots, the up-and-coming people, the insiders, the best. You are a cute, fat fellow, and we are going to put you on the right track."

Great. We left the shop, and began walking somewhere. We were having a good time, talking. These people treated me like a puppy they'd found. They were excited about what they were going to do for me. They talked about the place we were going. It was where the elite meet. They told me I'd never have found it on my own in a million years. It was where the brilliant met the soon-to-be-great and the almost famous met the nearly talented.

We got there. "This is it," my new friends said. "This is where it all happens."

It was a big bar and dance hall on the Lower East Side. It was crowded and noisy.

As we walked in, my college roommate, George, looked up from his beer. "Hi, Daniel," he said.

Eric, who'd lived across the hall, was dancing with my former girlfriend, Wendy. "Hi, Daniel," they said.

Peter Ryan was drinking at the bar. "Daniel!" he said. "We had some fun in art history class last year, didn't we?"

We moved through the place. At every table was someone I knew from college.

"These are the Young Turks? The movers and shakers?" I asked my new friends.

"The honor roll of talent, beauty and brains," they said. "This is the inside track."

I never did make contact with the big time. It does exist, doesn't it?

Mmmm! That's Prose!

Occasionally people tell me about creative writing classes, workshops and seminars for aspiring writers. The people telling me are usually awful writers, who can't and/or don't write.

What's more, some poor souls are addicted to attending this sort of thing, and do it over and over again.

Now this is something interesting you're unlikely to hear anywhere else: the people who teach creative writing usually can't write at all.

OK, I know there are exceptions. Don't sit down and write letters about the course you took with Vladimir Nabokov. I'm talking about the general condition. These guys can't write.

I had firsthand experience of this. I myself once filled in as a creative writing teacher at a local college. (I did a lousy job, incidentally.)

I met with the head of the English department—the very picture of a head of an English department—mellifluous, tweedy, intelligent-looking, used big words. Impressive.

He'd been teaching the advanced courses in creative writing for twenty years, but somehow had never made it into print. Maybe I'd be interested in seeing some of his work sometime. "Of course," I told him. "It really makes me mad how much good writing never gets published."

Well, he gave me a couple of stories. They were unbelievably bad. Painful. Ghastly. Horrible. There wasn't a paragraph, a sentence, not a word that could have been salvaged. Worse, he told me he'd been working on these very stories for a number of years.

He was a nice guy. What could I say to him? He was tone-deaf, color-blind, prose-lexic. I just avoided him until the end of the semester.

This guy was actually sort of innocent. He had no idea.

The kind of literary preceptor I dislike is the one who trumps up credentials and believes in his own authority. Here's a fellow whose poems have been published 172 times in various literary magazines. He's the real thing—who could doubt it? Of course, the whole time, he's been running his own literary magazine, in which he's published poems by the editors of all the magazines his stuff has appeared in. See how it works?

I'm mad at these birds because one of them told my wife to forget all about writing fiction—which was all she had ever wanted to do—not a speck of talent, no hope. And my wife listened to him. He brought Jill's writing to a dead stop.

Twenty years later, Jill figured out that what she'd been told was hogwash, and started turning out wonderful novels one after another.

Here's my policy regarding experts in creative writing: Ignore what they say. Ignore what they say when they tell you you're bad. Ignore what they say when they tell you you're good. It might be a good idea to ignore what I say too. May as well be thorough.

Gaudeamus Agita

In my first year of college, I was excited by everything the place offered. Everything interested me. I thought a lot about what was presented in classes, got into endless discussions with other students, and found things to read that weren't in the syllabus. I got C-minuses and D's, and couldn't understand why.

At the beginning of my second year, I got a new adviser. He explained how to succeed in school. Basically, he told me that I should find out exactly what each teacher wanted, and do it. It seemed sort of silly to me. I thought I was talented as a student. I had worked out a way to customize my education, and here this guy was telling me just to do the obvious thing. However, I was on academic probation by this time, so I agreed to give it a try.

I spent a lot of time looking things up in the index, reading pertinent paragraphs instead of whole books, and writing things down on 3-by-5 cards. I wrote papers that were boring and predictable. When the Dean's List came out, I was on it. I was making straight A's.

But I knew I had learned more the previous year, when I was doing lousy. It bugged me, and raised certain doubts. I quit school. I went home to Chicago and got a job. I also signed up for evening courses at the University of Chicago. I was going to take stuff just because it appealed to me, not to line up credits

161

for a degree. I took an art history course. It was more of an art appreciation course. It was a good course. The guy who taught it was named Harkin. I think he was a painter himself. He was enthusiastic. The other students were the usual assortment of people who take culture courses in night school: mostly adult learners seeking enrichment, like it says in the catalogue. I was the only actual kid.

What Harkin did was teach us how to look at paintings. He had a whole method. He showed us how to look at forms and color and line and composition. For assignments we had to go to the museum and draw diagrams of certain pictures, showing how the thing was organized. I really enjoyed myself. I'd had no idea that pictures could be seen like that. I went nuts when he showed us how there could be movement in a painting. He would show us how the painter had contrived that there would be a place in the picture to which your eye would first be drawn. From that point, the eye would be taken to another point, and then you'd start to take in textures, and colors. There could be rhythms in pictures, and harmonies and counterharmonies. I tell you, there was a lot to painting I had never known about.

Then came the big assignment. He turned us loose. Each of us was supposed to pick a painting and write about it. I was waiting outside the Art Institute when they unlocked the doors. I walked around and around, picking out my painting.

I picked a good one—"Excavation," by Willem DeKooning. It was a big sucker and plenty difficult. I gave it the double-O for a while, and then began scribbling in my notebook like mad. I had plenty to say about that picture. I analyzed the devil out of it. I wrote all about these cream-colored shapes that made a sort of screen or filigree in the foreground, and told how the shapes were reinforced with line, which created playful stresses and angularities. Operating behind this complex linear and mostly monochromic activity, areas of color were barely suggested, creating planar tension, and powerful sweeping movement. Listen—I wrote that painting up *good.* After filling up three or four pages, I just stood by and gazed at the thing—in case I had missed something. I really liked the painting by this time. I had a sort of proprietary feeling about it after doing all that analysis.

About this time the picture started to move. For real. And what was more, I wasn't looking at it from outside. I had been taken into the picture. I was being moved through it according to that internal logic that I had just been scribbling about. It took my breath away. It was exhilarating, and a little scary and hard to take. When the painting got done with me, and returned me to myself, I was a little shaken. I didn't hang around to see what else would happen. I thought it was time to get out of the museum.

So I went out of the museum, out onto Michigan Avenue. And all the buildings were paint. The cars going by—oh, the cars were wonderful—paint. The sky was paint. It was all paint, and texture, and colors going behind each other, and changing as they came next to each other. Even the air was paint, and I moved through it the way I had moved through the painting. I was a different kid in a different world.

I wrote my paper, but I didn't say anything about how the painting had picked me up and moved me around, or how it had been when I went outside the museum, and still was. That stuff was too personal to write about. So I stuck to the planar tensions and dynamic symmetry, and chromatic scheme.

A week or so later, Harkin flipped his wig. He was taking us through the museum. He was lecturing on modern sculpture. The class, the adult enrichment-seekers and I, were were standing around holding notebooks while he talked. I was trailing a little way behind the group, spacing out on a ceramic thing by Miró.

All of a sudden, Harkin was screaming. "You people ought to arrange to go and get yourselves buried somewhere!" he was yelling. "Because you're dead! Did you know that?"

As he stormed past me, he whispered, "Not you, kid. You're OK." He left the class standing there, and ran out of the Art Institute, onto Michigan Avenue, where cars, burnished black and red and brown, were moving like beetles across the bank of limestone skyscrapers, curving up into that cerulean sky with a grain like morocco leather.

Meet Me Under the
Cézanne, Poopsie

I used to hang around in the Museum of Modern Art, looking to meet girls.

"Do you like to have someone to talk to when you look at paintings?" I'd ask. "Or would you prefer to be by yourself?" Most of them said they didn't mind, and we'd walk around, discussing the art and sizing each other up.

Maybe we'd have coffee in the sculpture garden. It was a cheap impromptu date.

I would try to make a good impression. The rule is "Ask a lot of questions. Don't talk about yourself. Draw the other person out."

Of course, if the girl I'd just met in the museum asked me a lot of questions, and tried to draw me out, that would mean she was trying to make a good impression on me—and that was all right too.

I was developing some pretty smooth social skills.

One day, I met the ultimate, hanging out in the Museum of Modern Art, New York City, sophisticated, attractive—no, beautiful—girl. She had everything—wit, expensive clothes, bearing, education.

There we were, having coffee. I felt great. I felt as though I'd lived in New York, and done this sort of thing, all my life. I lit her cigarette. Urbane. Casual.

I didn't get to draw her out, though. She wasn't drawing me out, either. She was telling me about me.

"You've been in New York, what, six or eight months?"

"Seven."

"Where'd you go to school, St. Leon's College?"

"That's right! Amazing. Most people never heard of it. How'd you know that?"

"You look like a St. Leon's guy. Majored in art, I expect."

"Yeh, art."

"And now, you're doing pottery—no, printmaking, right?"

"Say, do you know me?"

"I'll bet you haven't missed any of the Kurosawa retrospective at the Toho Cinema."

"You saw me there, right?"

"Are you kidding? Favorite author Herman Melville?"

"Herman Melville."

"But you couldn't finish *Pierre*, right?"

"Right."

"Gonna write a novel yourself someday, aren't you? *Moby-Dick* as told by the whale, something like that."

"What are you, psychic?"

"No, I just come here a lot."

"What? You mean I'm a *type?*"

"Everybody's a type—but you're very nice."

"I don't suppose you'd like to see me again."

"I'd hate it."

"Of course."

She paid for my coffee and left. A valuable conversation, that. Most men are years older than I was when they find out that they're schnooks.

Talking to Kids

It may be that some of the people reading this have never read a book I've written. In that case, this will be particularly boring for you—so I'll tell you what to do:

Pretend that you have read a book of mine. Just pretend that you've read a certain book, and the characters are so real and so vivid that you feel like you know them. And the events of the story are so entertaining and you've thought about them so much that you feel as if they happened to you. What a good feeling!

Now imagine what a fantastic, brilliant fellow it would take to write a book that would make you feel like that. That's me. Some incredible guy.

For those of you who have read a book of mine, and do not feel that way about the book or me—you probably read the wrong book. Check the spelling of the author's name. Mine's P-i-n-k-w-a-t-e-r. A lot of names look like it.

OK, now on with the talk. Stories! Stories are neat. Don't you think so? Sure. We like stories. We use stories to communicate in our everyday life. When you meet someone, and want to get to know each other, the first thing you do is start telling stories about your lives: "Last summer, on our vacation, we went to the Grand Canyon, and I ate a hot dog and I got sick, and I threw up into the Grand Canyon."

Older people tell slightly different stories: "I had a tragic romance. She said she loved me, but she left me for a man who ran a hot dog wagon. I wanted to forget her, so I went to the Grand Canyon—but when I got there, instead of forgetting, I just threw up."

We also tell stories to explain things, or remind each other of points the stories illustrate.

"Remember the story of the boy who cried 'Wolf'?"

"No."

"Sure you do."

"I don't. Tell it to me."

"OK. Well, there was this boy . . . and he cried wolf. All day long he cried wolf up and down the streets . . . but nobody wanted to buy any of his wolves. So one day, he said to the wolves, 'I am going out of the wolf business. I am turning you loose. Fend for yourselves.' And the boy got a job selling hot dogs near the Grand Canyon. The wolves moved to Los Angeles and earned what they could.

"Later, the wolf craze, which goes on to this day, started, and wolves were selling for incredible prices. At the same time, a couple of local scandals involving bad hot dogs had caused the boy's business to fall off seriously.

"He became so depressed that he lost his footing, and fell most of the way down the Grand Canyon, breaking a number of his best bones, and wound up lodged in a thorny bush. The boy was miserable. 'I was a fool to turn those wolves loose so quick!' he cried."

"Is there a moral to this story?"

"Sure."

"What is it?"

"A fool and his wolf are soon parted."

So, you see, stories can be used to communicate or remind us of moral or philosophical wisdom.

Another kind of story we all tell is lies.

I never tell lies.

("He's lying.")

Look, I changed my mind. I don't feel like talking about stories anymore. I'm going to talk about something else. The reason I changed my mind is that this talk is supposed to be about changing your mind. That's what the people who asked me to do this said. Change your mind—that's the theme.

So I change my mind. I change the topic. I make it something else. I probably would have done that even if they hadn't asked me to.

Changing my mind is one of the things I do as a writer. It is basically what makes writing fun. See, I start out with some idea—and it doesn't matter what it is, because I know I'm going to change my mind at some point anyway. It can be an awful idea—and it usually is. It doesn't matter because I can always change it.

Does anybody remember the way they drew pictures when they were very small? Well, when you were very small, you just scribbled. It was hard enough to keep the point of the crayon on the paper. You just made scribbles—and that was very nice. I personally can remember some of my earliest scribbles.

After a while, when you're a little bit older, you try to do some more ambitious things as a scribbler. You might start choosing colors more consciously—or you might actually try to draw objects or people. But as a very little kid, you didn't have the coordination or experience to start right in drawing a realistic picture. Instead, you had to sort of work up speed by doing some scribbling—and then you'd add a head and feet, for example. Or you might be fine on feet and a hat—but you'd run out of technique after that, and fill in the rest with scribbling.

What I want to talk about in particular is when you start out with a scribble and then see that it looks like something. When adults doodle, they do this—and I believe most kids go through a period of drawing this way. If you haven't done this, or don't remember doing it, I suggest you try it. You'll get some surprising results. This sort of thing is related to looking at clouds and imagining that they're horses or whales or a map of New Jersey.

When I set out to write a story, I usually begin with an idea—any old idea—it doesn't matter what. Maybe it isn't even an idea as such, but just a line, or a character, or a situation. It doesn't matter, because I know I'm going to change my mind.

I'm going to quit fooling around now. I really know what they mean by "change your mind." It's not "change your mind" in the sense of picking something else to write about or think about—although I think it's really good to do that.

What they really want me to talk about is having an experience that makes your mind different—having something happen after which you yourself are changed. This really happens—in fact, it happens all the time.

I should say, it tries to happen all the time—we aren't always in the right mood for it to happen. I think this is something very personal and special, this changing of mind. I don't know just how it works—but it has certainly happened to me more than once.

I remember looking at the full moon and storm clouds on a windy night. I looked for a long time. It was a really amazing night. I got to know a lot of things about how things looked, just by looking so hard. And things have never looked exactly the same since.

I also remember looking for a long time at a painting called *Excavation*, by Willem De Kooning, in a museum. I got very interested in that picture—then I got very excited about it—and I got the feeling that I was moving around inside the picture. I think the artist intended that I should feel that way. It was exciting and a little scary for me. When I went out of the museum, the way things looked made sense to me in a whole different way. Everything still looks a little different to me since that time.

I remember when my mind was changed by learning to read. I happen to remember the exact moment when I learned to read—I mean, really knew I was able to read. I was a first grader, and I had bought a *Batman* comic book. I think it may have been the first brand-new comic I ever bought. I was determined to read the whole thing—and I did. I even remember the very pictures, and what Batman was saying—complicated stuff, things that were not in the first-grade reader. "Hey! I can read this!" I said. "I can read anything!" That changed my mind in a big way.

But the *Batman* comic was not like the painting by Willem DeKooning. It was not the intention of the comic-book artists and writers to change my mind. They were just doing a job, and making something entertaining. It wasn't supposed to be Art (with a big A).

It can be funny what changes your mind. Sometimes, like with the comic book, art (with a small A) can do it. Some people have a favorite song that makes them feel really special. Some people can remember a certain cheeseburger they ate twenty years ago that made them understand what life was all about. All sorts of things can change your mind.

But if you want to change your mind. If you get so you like the feeling of all sorts of new ideas and ways to look at things and think about things crowding in and mixing you up, and making life interesting—then your best bet is Art (with a big A). That's what it's for.

Most of the time, I try to be a writer of books that are Art (with a big A). I don't know when I've done it, because it's a tricky, sneaky, hard-to-define sort of thing. I don't think a writer can start out saying, "This will be the big A kind of book. This will get people's minds changing." I usually can tell when someone has had that in mind, and I usually don't finish the book—it never seems to work for me when it's so purposeful.

I think some of my books are big A books because people who have read them often write me letters saying they've read a particular book fifteen or sixteen times, and they think about it all the time. Other people send me things they've written—they say they've written these things because they keep thinking about some book or books I've written. After a while, I think I've probably made a big A sort of book.

It's hard to tell what is big A art and what is small A art. For one thing, big A artists make small A art sometimes, and you never know when a small A artist will turn out something that is big A. I'm not sure it even matters.

The only reason I'm talking about this is that I want to warn everybody to be very mistrustful of people who claim to know which is which. They usually don't know anything. Sorry—but it's true. The people who have to do with books—picking them, publishing them, selling them and talking about them (and that includes me for today only)—have a way of treating everything like big A art and making sure it's small A art. They may mean well, but you can't trust them.

The only way to find books (and other things) that are apt to be mind-changing, big A experiences is to look at and listen to and read *everything*. This takes time, but if you cut down on television, which is small A anyway, you can do it. You yourself have to find the stuff you can use to change your mind. That's if you want it changed. It isn't compulsory. Of course, an unchanged mind is a little like unchanged underwear. It tends to get unattractive even to the person whose mind or underwear it is.

Guy Talk

Athrilling story of the high-powered world of children's publishing. And how I found out about sexism.

At the time I'm telling about, I was doing my usual thing, which is writing kids' books. I had just handed in a book in which a character—I think it was a turtle—was telling tall tales, and he claimed to have once been President of the United States. He said something like "I used to be President of the United States. In those days I went by the name of Dwight D. Eisenhower." Just a little minor aside. Not important.

The editor called me up and said, "We can't have this. I think it's against the law to be disrespectful to the President of the United States."

"There's nothing disrespectful about it," I said. "Besides, Eisenhower isn't President anymore."

"Just the same, let's be on the safe side and take it out."

"You're telling me that my turtle can't say that he was once Dwight D. Eisenhower?"

"That's right."

"Because some people might take it seriously?"

"It's disrespectful."

Maybe she's an Eisenhower fan, I thought. "What if I had him say he used to be Lyndon Johnson?"

"No. Just leave it out."

173

There was nothing out of the ordinary about this exchange. This is the level on which children's books are frequently edited, and one sort of learns to put up with it.

This particular time, it bugged me.

A couple of days later, I was in New York City, with a few hours to kill. I was in the neighborhood, and I thought I'd go up to the publishers' and make a scene. I was still mad about that idiocy about the turtle.

I appeared in the office and demanded to see my editor. I was going to fuss and fume, and maybe snatch my manuscript away. It turned out the editor was out of the office that day.

"Well, just get me my manuscript—I've had all I can stand."

"Maybe, you'd like to talk to Mr. Nate."

Mr. Nate was the supreme boss. I'd never met him.

"Yes. I want to see Mr. Nate."

I was escorted to Mr. Nate's office.

"Mr. Pinkwater, please sit down," Mr. Nate said.

I sat down.

"Mr. Pinkwater, I understand you're having a little difficulty with one of my editors."

"Well, yes."

"Mr. Pinkwater, you're a man of the world, and I'm a man of the world. I know you'll understand this. This office is like a little family. And I'm the father to all these females."

I should explain that children's book editors are predominantly women.

"I have to keep things running smoothly. I know the girls get silly ideas into their heads—but we have to make concessions to the fair sex, don't we?"

By this time, I'm thanking God for letting me hear this speech. I never dreamed anybody actually talked this way. I've changed the names and circumstances to protect the innocent—namely, me—but Mr. Nate's remarks are verbatim.

"Women, God bless them, we can't live with them and we can't live without them. Isn't that right, Mr. Pinkwater?"

"Sure, Mr. Nate."

"I'll smooth out your little difficulty with your editor, and the next time you have a problem, you just walk past all those little offices, and come here to the big office. How would you like that?"

"Gee, Mr. Nate," I said, "that would be swell."

I quit publishing with that outfit. I didn't have the heart to fight with my editor after meeting her boss.

One thing I never have been able to work out—was the editor an idiot because she was an idiot, or because it was expected of her?

I'm sure things have changed since then. Haven't they?

Ideas and How to Fix Them

I get a fair amount of mail from readers. Most of them are kids—which makes sense, since the books I write are kids' books—but adults write too.

In general adults write to make statements, and kids write to ask questions. This, in a nutshell, is why I prefer writing for kids.

The letters from adults tend to fall into two categories. They want to congratulate me on having done a good job, or they want to upbraid me for having committed what they consider a sin.

Should I make even passing mention of a witch or a werewolf, or especially the devil, I can count on hearing from people who accuse me of being in league with the powers of darkness. I am also notified of other errors. Recently, I got a letter from a naval officer who said that my contention that balsa and tissue paper model airplanes are better than plastic kits was the equivalent of a sexist or racial slur. I love adults. They're so sensible.

Now the kids' letters. They're a big part of the payoff for being a kids' author. These kids are great! I know we are supposed to be hurtling into the great darkness of illiteracy. TV has ruined the minds of three generations. Our values stink. We're sinking into a swamp of incompetency.

But you couldn't prove any of this by my correspondence.

176

Just about every day I get a letter from someone who is just discovering language, and is having fun with it, and wants to share the fun with me. The kid has read something, enjoyed it, figured out how it's done, and is sending me a sample. Mostly pretty good, these samples. Some get quite elaborate, with suggestions, additional chapters, jokes and drawings.

In the simplest form, there are just a bunch of questions. How many books have you written? How long does it take to write one? Do you have any pets? Where do you get your ideas?

Where do you get your ideas? That's the most frequently asked question. And it happens to be one I have trouble with. I'm not sure I understand it. Sometimes I just write back that I don't know. Or I give a string of examples of where ideas might come from—news stories, personal experience, stories people tell me, dreams. I never really feel that I've handled it well.

It may be that I'm confused by the way the question is framed. It suggests that one *gets* ideas from *somewhere*. I'd have an easier time if the question were "How do you develop ideas?"

Ideas come ten a minute—to everybody. Most of them aren't much good—initially—at least mine aren't. It seems to me the trick is to develop them, and improvise on them. I'm thinking about the way musicians learn to take a theme and fool around with it, work changes on it, and bring it along. Clearly, it takes talent—but it's also something you learn by doing a lot.

Sometimes I think that inspiration is really just a sort of speeded-up or concentrated process of tinkering. We hear all these stories about how Mozart or Beethoven could be given a theme and sit down and knock out a bunch of terrific variations. If they'd said, "Let me take this home for a couple of months, and work on it," the story wouldn't be as impressive, though the variations might be.

When you read something in a book, you're confronted by

the finished product—it's as though the author has just knocked it off, at the same rate at which you're reading it. "How did he do it? Where does he get these ideas?"

Of course, Mozart was able to do this stuff off the cuff when he was six years old—something a person who gets letters from literate kids can appreciate.

You ought to see how those kids take off on my stories. Where do I get my ideas? Are they kidding?

Chiaroscuro

I walk into the office of an editor in a publishing house in New York City. He's got *The New York Times* spread out on his desk. He's drinking a cup of coffee.

He's glad to see me, of course. Someone to talk to while he waits for lunchtime to roll around. I get comfortable. We're chatting away. There are pauses wherein we look out the window at the inspiring skyline. I'm used to the routine—stretch it out, pass the time. If he doesn't already have a lunch date with an author, there may be a plate of chow mein in the offing, if I play my cards right.

I hear a sound in the corridor. Squeak, squeak, squeak. The editor perks up. He gets an alert expression. He's watching the door.

Squeak, squeak, squeak.

A fellow wearing a raincoat and carrying a big zipper portfolio appears in the doorway. He's wearing those ripple sole shoes, the kind postmen wear. Squeak, squeak, squeak.

"Hey, Fred!" the editor calls.

The squeaker pauses. He looks in at the doorway. "Yes, Jim?"

"Say Fred, can you draw muskrats?"

"Muskrats? Sure."

"We've got a manuscript about muskrats," Jim says. "Tell Susan I said to give it to you."

"OK, Jim."

Squeak, squeak, squeak. The guy in the raincoat leaves.

"Who was that?" I ask.

"That's Fred Chiaroscuro," the editor says. He does a lot of work for us."

A lot was putting it mildly. I later found out that Fred illustrated about 40 children's books a year to the tune of maybe a couple thousand dollars each time.

Days he would trudge around the publishing houses, squeak, squeak, squeak. Nights he would draw like a fiend.

Meanwhile, all these publishers would have one day a week set aside for looking at the work of illustrators. Some poor devil employed by the publisher would draw the assignment and have to sit at a desk making encouraging remarks about portfolios brought in by one hopeful artist after another. They'd dutifully take down the address and phone number of each artist, and put it in a file that was never looked at again.

And when the editor needed pictures? Right. Fred. This accounts for why children's books all looked alike for a certain period. Fred wasn't much of an artist, but he had legs like a horse.

I think the point is clear to the aspirant. It's the squeaking illustrator that gets the job.

And the Voice of the Snerd'll
Be Heard in the Land

A vast number of kids' books gets published every year. The majority of them you will not find in your local bookshop. Most kiddie publishers don't even try for retail sales—they specialize in sales to schools and libraries.

Every school and library system reviews books for purposes of deciding what to buy. The reviews are written by your children's teachers and librarians.

Some of the publishers collect these reviews and, in a desultory way, send batches of photocopies to the author.

I'm going to quote from a bunch of these, just to give you the flavor.

They're all responses to a book of mine, *The Muffin Fiend*, published a year or two ago by Lothrop, Lee & Shepard.

This one says: *"The only thing interesting in this book was the illustrations. They seemed to be done with computer graphics. The story was ridiculous."*

Here's another: *"Bound sturdily, but has an ugly cover."*

And *"The illustrations were not clear enough for young children who cannot interpret unclear images. The muffins in this book were a mystery even to me because their shape was not what I pictured a muffin to be."*

Well, some people can draw muffins—some can't.

Here's one from someone who liked the book, but can't write

an English sentence: *"His icon is Mozart, from which he was inspired to write about when seeing his suit at the age of nine."*

I like this reviewer a little better: *"With Paris and Vienna muffinless, it is up to W. A. Mozart to 'figaro' how to catch the elusive Don Pastrami who is stealing all the muffins."*

Here's one written by a parent volunteer: *"A funny book, easy to read, with black and white computer drawings on each page."* A "Media Specialist" (that's a librarian) from the same system writes: *". . . will appeal to fans, but will leave others confused."*

Look! Here's someone who loved it: *"Perhaps it could spark some interest in who Mozart really was or where Vienna is . . . it will definitely tickle a child's funny bone. A great summer reading book!"*

Here's someone who's just about had it with me: *"This wild and disjointed mystery will not make sense to kids. I hope Pinkwater will invent something really creative again, before we have to write a Requiem for Pinkwater."*

Many of the reviews are simply little forms filled out with check marks—recommended, not recommended, and so forth.

This is one I like: *"The characters left me cold and the children will not understand the humor. They will most likely not know who Mozart is, or care. Because of the difficulty of his name, they will probably just skip over it and will not understand the absurdity of the idea. The French names and Austrian phrases will only serve to make it more difficult to read for children.*

"Finally, despite the silly idea of an extraterrestrial (and what child will be able to read that word?) using muffins to fuel his spaceship, why in the world does it have to look like the Washington Monument? It is just one more obscure thing in a sadly silly book."

A sadly silly book.

Here's an *educated* librarian, Annette Curtis Klause, writing in *School Library Journal:* *"Pinkwater's audience realizes that* often there is more there than meets the eye, and feels pleased to be entrusted with these mystical items that will one day burst deliciously like sherbet-centered candy when the reference is recognized."

Finally, here is Eric Faller, Grade 4, writing in the *Asbury Park Press*, Asbury Park, New Jersey:

"*The first thing I noticed about this book is the pictures. I like the way the pictures were made with dots. I also liked the story.*

"*The Muffin Fiend takes place in Europe a long time ago and all the muffins are disappearing. Two people find the muffin fiend by playing a small violin. They also find out that he is not from this planet, but if you want to know how he gets here you should read it for yourself. You can even sing part of this book. I think it was an exciting story.*"

Novel idea, having a kid review kids' books.

Skivvies Make the Man

The producer of "All Things Considered" told me that he'd be happy with anything I might do in the way of commentaries, as long as I didn't start writing pieces for radio about writing pieces for radio. He doesn't want any self-referential stuff. In principle, I agree with him.

On the other hand, ever since he told me that, I've been compulsively thinking about what sort of piece one could write for radio about writing a piece for radio. It's begun to bug me. I have to do it.

Maybe they'll put this on as a horrible example for other commentators.

Anyway—I have to get this off my mind, so I can go on to other things.

This is how I do a commentary, including this one you're listening to now.

To start with, I sit in front of the computer. This can go on for hours. I used to sit in front of the typewriter before I caught up with the technological revolution. I don't switch the computer on, because there's a little fan inside that hisses. It annoys me. When I do get around to switching it on, I type as fast as I can and mash down hard on the keys so that the clicking noise will drown out the fan.

It gets deadly boring, sitting in front of an unswitched-on

computer. To inspire myself, I listen to folk music, most of which I detest, on the local college FM station. The sound of people clawing at guitars, and singing songs that go on forever, puts me in mind of the fact that culture is at a low ebb, and this gives me courage to switch on the computer and start to write. How much worse can I do than a Vassar student playing the banjo?

The next thing I have to pay attention to is making the thing come out between one and three minutes. Sometimes they can get as long as four minutes. A double-spaced page is equivalent to about a minute.

The caterwauling of the folksingers and having to pay attention to the length fully occupies my mind, which means I haven't much attention left for what I'm actually writing. Experience has demonstrated that this approach brings good results. I'm not at my best when I know what I'm talking about.

After a while, I notice I'm somewhere into page three, and it's time to wind the thing up. Then comes the nice part about writing on a computer. I whiz up and down in the text, trying to find and take out things that look especially stupid. When I've taken out the worst parts, I turn the printer on. The pages clatter out.

Next I have to record it. I shut the windows to get rid of noise of birds and dogs, and cars going by.

I hook up the microphone and the tape recorder. I went out and bought semiprofessional equipment. I got it at one of those discount places. They will not be undersold. I think I got a good deal.

All the commentaries so far have been done in warm weather. My office is at the top of the house, and it's pretty hot even with the windows open. Once I've got them closed, the next thing I do is rip off my clothes.

This is the sort of detail one inevitably comes to in writing this sort of piece. This is why the producer warned me not to do one. It can't help a serious news and information program for the listeners to know that commentaries are being recorded by a guy in an attic, in his underwear.

The exciting part of doing the taping is to try to get it right before I suffocate, and before a big truck rumbles by and the microphone picks it up.

Well, it looks like I've nailed down another one. I love doing this. I wonder why I didn't get into show business sooner.

Who's Little Jackson Pollock
Are You?

I had a number of jobs teaching art to kids in various settlement houses, community summer programs, and the like.

I found out a good deal about what's involved in teaching art to kids. It's fairly simple, but hardly anyone does it right.

Here's the whole thing in a nutshell. The first thing you need to know is that visual expression—drawing and painting and so forth—is a natural part of human communication, just like speaking and reading. The difference is, we expect everybody to learn to speak and read, but we make a special case for art. Some have talent, and some don't. The ones that don't, or appear not to, are systematically discouraged from trying to do art.

There have been societies in which everybody did everything. Eskimos, for example. In the old days, an Eskimo would make a walrus-bone spoon, first killing the walrus and winding up by carving the decorations on the handle. He didn't worry if he had talent or not. You can see the spoons in museums. The standard is pretty high.

Having figured this out, I decided that my first goal as an art teacher would be to undo, or at least de-emphasize, whatever conventional pressures these kid artists were usually made to feel.

The way I handled this was to say as little as possible and to keep the rules of the art room to a minimum. I boiled them down

187

to two: (1) No violence, and (2) Pinkwater will hand out paints. Both of these rules were of a practical nature. Excessive high spirits meant that paint would fly, and I'd be put to expense to have my clothes cleaned. Rule 2, that I'd spoon the tempera paint out of the quart jars onto their little pallets, the same— also it gave me some contact with the kids and a plausible reason for being there.

For the rest, I mainly kept my mouth shut, except when I was spoken to. I responded to direct questions. If no one talked to me, I'd stand around looking pleasant, handing out the paint. After the class had gotten going, new kids who drifted in would have the rules explained to them by the kids who were already there, so they didn't have to talk to me at all until they were ready.

When a new kid came into the class, he'd spend the first two or three sessions trying to figure out what I wanted him to do so he could do it and get adult approval. The kid would do his best stock painting and bring it over to me and show it to me. "Do you like my painting?"

"Sure. Do you like it?"

"Well . . . yes."

"Good. That's all that matters. You want to take it home or keep it here?" Or I might say, "You need any more paint?"

"What should I paint now?"

"You can paint anything you like."

After a while, they'd start to catch on. The best single moment I remember was a kid who asked me, "Pinkwater, are you a real art teacher?"

"What do you think?"

"I think you're just someone who likes kids' paintings."

"That's exactly right."

I had set up a corner where kids could throw paint. If a kid told me he or she didn't know what to do, I'd suggest the kid try tossing some paint. There was a 30" by 40" sheet of chip board leaning against the wall, and I'd clip a big sheet of paper to it, and show the kid how to mix a little paint with water in a paper cup and toss it underhand at the paper. The result was a neat splash and dribble. The different colors would slop over each other and make new colors. Often, the kids would take the paper to their easels and paint with brushes over the tossed paint.

One girl had a session of paint throwing and got interested in the interaction of colors. She asked me questions about mixing colors, and I answered them. The next day she announced that she was going to do a painting with nine kinds of pink. She managed to come up with seven. I figure she learned most of what there is to know about color theory.

I loved it when the kids would whisper to each other about me. "Don't worry about him. He doesn't care what you paint." To test this, every kid would try a scatological or sacrilegious subject to see if I would react any differently. I didn't.

A bunch of little boys got into painting nudes—completely from imagination with breasts like faucets. The next day I brought in a bunch of museum postcards of nudes and pinned them up before the class. The boys studied them—sort of reverentially. Then they went back to painting spaceships and airplanes. For some reason, that was a specially quiet and peaceful day in the art room.

This is an actual dialogue I overheard between two of the kids:

"What's that you're painting?"

No reply.

"Is it a clown? It looks like a clown."

"No, it's not a clown."

"Is it a butterfly? It could be a butterfly."

"It's not a butterfly."

"Well what is it then?"

"It's a Japanese motorcycle."

"That's not a motorcycle! It doesn't look anything like a motorcyle to me!"

"It doesn't have to. It's my picture."

I taught those kids a lot without saying much.

Oh yes, and I never made the kids clean up the room. I did that after they left. It was the least I could do for them, considering all they were teaching me.

I Worketh 9 to 5

Once I had a job on a production line. What I had to do was grab this stuff from my left, drag it over to my right, stop at the mark, and pull the lever. Then I did it again.

It was grab, drag, stop, pull—grab, drag, stop, pull—starting at 7:30 in the morning, with a half-hour for lunch and two five-minute breaks. It was not a job you could love.

But I found a way to love it. I had never handed in my senior English textbook from high school. Every night I would cut out a poem. I'd bring the poem to work in my pocket, also a roll of Scotch tape.

First thing, I'd tape the poem to my machine, the one with the lever. From starting time until lunch, while doing my work, I'd read the poem—memorize it. When lunchtime came, I'd peel the poem off the machine, and from the end of lunch until quitting time, I'd recite the poem, and the other poems I'd learned, in my head.

So it was:

> *grab, drag, stop, pull*
>   Orpheus with his lute made trees
> *grab, drag, stop, pull*
>   And the mountain tops that freeze
> *grab, drag, stop, pull*

191

Bow themselves when he did sing:
grab, drag, stop, pull
To his music plants and flowers
grab, drag, stop, pull
Ever sprung; as sun and showers
grab, drag, stop, pull
There had made a lasting spring.
grab, drag, stop, pull
Every thing that heard him play,
grab, drag, stop, pull
Even the billows of the sea,
grab, drag, stop, pull
Hung their heads and then lay by.
grab, drag, stop, pull

Pretty soon, the boss called me into the office.

"This is probably the first time you've ever been fired. I'm sure this is upsetting to you, and you're wondering if you're even able to keep a job. I want you to know that I think you're a nice boy, and you'll be a good worker in the future—but I can't have you here anymore."

"But why? Did I do something wrong?"

"You're weird is why," the boss said. "It's that goofy smile on your face. You look like you're in love all the time. When I walk down the line, everybody looks right—like they belong here—like they're working. And there you are, with that goony smile. It makes me nervous."

So I got fired. I walked out of there into the midmorning sunlight. I can't say it bothered me much.

In sweet music is such art,
Killing care and grief of heart.
Fall asleep, or hearing, die.

PART SIX

JUST THE FUNDAMENTALS

Give the People Cartoons
They Can Whistle

I received a phone call one evening.

"Pinky baby! We're going to revolutionize Saturday morning television!"

"What are we going to do, blow up the transmitter? Who is this?"

"It's Pudovkin. We're gonna work together. You're a genius, Pinky baby!"

"Pudovkin?"

"I love you, Pinky. I love your books!"

"Which ones in particular?"

"What?"

"Which books of mine do you love?"

"Who knows? Books! Titles! There's money in this. We're going to do great things."

"Is this a prank!"

"Is this a prank! The guy's hilarious! What a riposte! What wit! Oh, Pinky! You're brilliant!"

"Who gave you my phone number?"

"Saul Bellow. Saul says you're the only man who can do the job I have in mind."

"Saul Bellow knows who I am?"

"He loves you, baby!"

"Saul Bellow, the big writer?"

195

"We're going to do something incredible, Pink!"

"Saul Bellow said you should call me?"

"And am I glad he did. You're everything he said you were."

"This is a television show we're talking about?"

"Like nothing ever seen before. And Pink . . ."

"Yes?"

"I consider you a close personal friend."

"Well . . . that's . . . uh . . . very nice."

"We'll be in touch. Never change, Harvey."

"It's Daniel."

"Right. Love ya, Harvey baby."

"Gee. Saul Bellow?"

That was how I got hired to develop the revolutionary new children's TV show, "Fuzzy Bunny Babies."

Of course, I had many conversations and meetings with Elvis Pudovkin. A genius.

One of the first conversations was about the title.

"Elvis, are you sure you want to call this thing 'Fuzzy Bunny Babies'? "

"You don't like it, Harvey?"

"Well, it sounds sort of dippy."

"Strategy, Harvey baby. We have to lull them into a false sense of security."

"Why do we have to lull them?"

"These network guys have no talent. We have to make them think the show is junk. Then they'll buy it."

"Why do we want to make junk?"

"We don't, Harvey. Once they commit to the series, we'll stick in the quality. Leave this part to me. I'm good in offices."

Elvis apparently knew what he was doing. The television network did indeed commission an outline, then a script sample, then a script. Elvis was happy. He continued to call me Harvey.

Elvis taught me a lot. He explained how the network would expect me to work certain objects into the stories.

"What objects?"

"Well, you know, objects. Oh, say one of the bunnies has a certain kind of weapon."

"Weapon? These are fuzzy bunnies! What do they need with weapons?"

"It's the toy companies. They'd like it if the bunnies used products."

"Hey, I'm not going to do that!"

"Just until we get started, Harvey. We'll pull a fast one. Once we're in production we'll do it just like—what's that book you were telling me about—*The Wind in the Willows*? Meanwhile, I want you should watch the 'Smurfs.' Make ours more like the 'Smurfs.' 'Smurfs' is a big hit."

The network assigned two executives to work with us. We had a conference call.

"We're very excited about the show," the two executives said. "We hope we can work closely with you."

"Listen. Don't worry about Pinky," Elvis said. "He's a little weird, but I can control him, right, Harvey?"

"Right, Elvis," I said.

At the last minute, the network dropped "Fuzzy Bunny Babies." They chose a show called "Space Otters" instead.

Elvis took it like a man. He said it was all my fault, but that I shouldn't feel bad. He had two shows in development with the other networks.

And so, he passed from my life. Farewell, Elvis Pudovkin, great spirit, genius. I am honored to have come as close as I did to helping enrich our nation's culture.

It Hurts Here. And Here. And Here.

I have a fashionable disease. Chronic fatigue syndrome. It's all the rage.

Not everybody can have this disease. To qualify, you have to have eight out of eleven of the following symptoms: mild fever, sore throat, painful lymph nodes, generalized muscle weakness, muscle discomfort, headaches, painful joints, sleep problems, sudden onset of the symptoms, and trouble concentrating, confusion and forgetfulness. I've got 'em all.

The other main feature is that it takes all day to recover if you overexert, if you have a mild case, such as mine. People who have it worse can really suffer.

What's more, your doctor has to rule out a whole list of other, pretty serious illnesses which may have similar symptoms. I've got it for sure. It comes and goes. It isn't curable. It isn't fatal.

It used to be referred to as the "yuppie disease," which is fairly annoying to one of my temperament and backgound.

But I am not complaining about having the disease. I sort of like it. I like it because it permits me to cop out on a greater scale than ever before. I cancel out of social events without guilt. I leave boring parties early. I insist that business meetings take place in my neighborhood in the country rather than schlep into the city.

"Look, I'm a sick man. I have to conserve energy." Everyone feels sorry for me, or at least defers to me.

I also like my disease because of my nature, which is cheerfully fatalistic. I'd rather have a light touch of yuppie disease than AIDS, cancer, depression, alcoholism or kidney disease, to name a few.

Which brings me to my theory of displaced suffering. This is based on the obvious fact that each life can encompass only so much pain and aggravation. If you're fully occupied with one sort of misery, it is unlikely that anything else will bother you.

I discovered this theory, and how to harness its power, the first time I owned a French car. It was a Peugeot, but it could have been any make.

If you are the owner of a French automobile, other sources of unhappiness will recede. Except for a certain awkwardness in getting from place to place, your life will be an endless song of joy.

When I owned the Citroën, every human was my friend, every day—as long as I didn't try to drive anywhere—a span of perfect happiness. And in the period during which I held title to two Renaults, I never so much as caught a cold.

I suppose I could kick this chronic fatigue syndrome if I went over to Left Bank Imported Cars and made a deal—but I'll live with the symptoms for the present.

Better the yuppie you know.

Jolie Voiture

Y ou know, you can think you're really over it. Everything is going along fine. Your life is OK. Getting along with people. Doing your work. Years can pass. You never give it a thought. And then, all of a sudden . . .

COMPULSION.

It happens. It happened to me.

I started thinking about buying a French car.

This friend of mine . . . sent me a . . . a brochure. Some guy in California . . . is importing the Citroën Deux Chevaux. That cute little thing—looks like a Volkswagen, but its got little headlights, little bug-eye headlights, sitting up on top of the fenders. The top rolls back. You can unscrew the seats, with wingnuts, and take them out and have a picnic. It's got a two-cylinder, air-cooled engine. They're really wonderful. I mean . . . I really want one.

I was told by a regional representative of another make of French car that the way they safety test cars in France is . . . they don't use dummies. They use cadavers. It's . . . uh . . . more scientific, he said.

"Hev we completed ze test of ze new model 409?"

"Yes, we hev."

"And, ah, how are ze subjects?"

"Mmm, they seem to be dead."

"Ah yes, but are they any more dead than before ze experiment?"

"Nnn, no, I would say they are just about precisely as dead as before."

"So, ah, ze crash had no discernible effect on them?"

"Mmm, none that we can really ascertain, no."

"So I guess it would be correct to say that this car is completely safe in case of an impact, yes?"

"Mm, yes, zat would be a fair assumption."

"It's another masterpiece of engineering. I will make my report to the marketing department."

I'm thinking about donating my body to the Department of Automotive Engineering at some university.

Three Years Ago I Couldn't
Spell Engineer

I thought I'd try one of those lighthearted consumer topics. You ever see that guy on television—the one who brings in bunches of products and makes cute remarks about what it says on the labels? This is going to be like that.

I like to have something to sip when I'm working at my desk. I buy seltzer in ten-ounce bottles. They come in six-packs— six bottles held together by a sort of plastic cowling into which the necks of the bottles are inserted. You've seen those plastic things. They're always finding them in the stomachs of dead walruses.

The bottles themselves have screw-off caps that are a masterpiece of engineering. The caps are made of aluminum, or some other light alloy. The caps are shaped to wrap around the neck of the bottle, which, in addition to having a screw thread, has a molded shoulder, or boss, or retaining ring toward the bottom of the neck.

The part of the cap that wraps around this ring is divided into eight segments, which are attached to the main body of the cap by sixteen tiny welds. Near the top of the cap are twenty perforations, just below the level of the plastic seal, which is on the inside of the cap.

When the cap is deployed a number of things happen. During the initial quarter-turn of the cap counterclockwise, the eight segments at the bottom of the cap move slightly outward, thus releasing their grip around the boss. At the same time, the twenty perforations move above the level of the mouth of the bottle, allowing an initial release of gases and reducing the probability of a pressure malfunction.

In the course of the second quarter-turn, the eight curved segments move apart and outward, clearing the retaining ring and allowing full deployment. At this point the twenty perforations are no longer functional, and further excessive pressure is released around the entire surface of the inside of the cap, causing a light spray of seltzer all over the papers on my desk.

The bottles are inserted so tightly in the walrus-killer that one has to twist them out with some force. This tends to dislodge one or more of the eight retaining segments, which then function like woodcarvers' gouges.

When I go to unscrew the thing, it usually takes a slice a little under an eighth of an inch wide and a half-inch long out of the palmar surface of the second phalange of my middle finger.

When I remember, I put on a heavy-duty leather work glove when I open these, or use an adjustable wrench. There are no safety instructions printed on the indestructible polyvinyl foam combination label and bottle-protector.

What was wrong with those things you pried off, the ones with the little disk of cork inside?

Polychromics

I'll bet you thought I was just a zany. Not so. Here's me taking a stand on one of the vital issues of the day:

I am in favor of colorization. You know what is it, colorization? It's that process by which black-and-white film is run through a computer, and it comes out in color.

Many people are horrifed by this practice. They claim it's a violation of the integrity of the filmmaker.

I think it's great. Here's why: when they colorize a film they have to get hold of a really good black-and-white print—no scratches, nice and crisp. So the film is conserved. Then they use the colorized version strictly for television, broadcast, or videocassette.

There's a little wheel just under the screen on my television set. You turn it all the way to the left, and guess what you get? Black and white!

Get it? You aren't obliged to watch *Rashomon* in lurid color. Just turn the little wheel. Or watch it in color if you want to. I'm happy these old movies will be broadcast late at night, and available at the video shop. I'll be viewing in mono.

Some films don't suffer when they're colorized. Laurel-and-Hardys are just fine in color. I've seen some. And in fact, the daughter of one of them said she wished the boys could come back to see the color versions. She said they'd just love them.

Some stuff is so good you can't ruin it. Like Bach played on a synthesizer.

Speaking of Laurel and Hardy, I was quoted on the subject. A film critic wrote that the best paragraph of the year, about film, did not appear in a film journal, but in a kids' book. People are always surprised when they find something worthwhile in a kids' book.

The truth is, I had no idea I'd written something intelligent. If the paragraph was good enough to appear in a respected film magazine, I see no reason not to quote it here:

"The thing about Laurel and Hardy movies that you can't get from the chopped-up versions on television is how beautiful they are. Things happen exactly at the moment they have to happen. They don't happen a second too soon or too late. You can even predict what's going to happen—and it does happen—and it surprises you anyway. It doesn't surprise you because it happened, but because it happened so perfectly."

[ANNOUNCER VOICE]

The passage Mr. Pinkwater read was from his novel The Snark-out Boys and the Avocado of Death. Still available in black and white.

All Bash and No Brains

Some time ago, I had a conversation with a kid about to graduate from college. It was my college—the one I'm careful never to name. This kid was an art major. Sculpture was his thing.

"So what kind of sculpture are you interested in?" I asked him.

"What do you mean, 'what kind of sculpture'? Sculpture. I'm a sculptor."

"I mean, what sculpture do you like?"

"Mine. I like my sculpture."

"Good for you. But I was trying to find out what sculptors you like. Other than yourself."

"Besides me?"

"That's right."

"There's Fred."

"Fred?"

"He's a good sculptor. And Louis. Louis is good too."

"You're talking about friends of yours, am I right?"

"Well, Fred is more my friend than Louis—but I respect Louis also."

"What I wanted to find out was what sculptors do you like whose work I might know."

"I don't know. What sculptors do you know?"

"Ever hear of Rodin?"

"No."

"Henry Moore, Jacques Lipshitz, Alexander Calder?"

"No."

"Gutzon Borglum, Ossip Zadkine, Daniel Chester French, Brancusi, Giacometti, Gislebertus, Michelangelo?"

"Who are those, old-time guys?"

"You've never been in a museum, have you?"

"What for? I don't want to look at old dead guys' stuff. It would corrupt my vision."

I remember that I was something of an arrogant putz myself when I was this kid's age, but he surpassed me. I couldn't help wondering whether his militant ignorance was a pose. Or that the militancy was a pose. The ignorance appeared to be real. A classmate of mine, who is now a professor, told me that his main concern with undergraduates is dealing with their feelings of inferiority to those generations of students that preceded them— ones who had read more than three books before coming to college. My friend is of the opinion that the kids he deals with feel personally responsible for knowing almost nothing. They don't see it as characteristic of their entire generation. He sees his job as comforting them, and persuading them that it isn't too late.

"So you start reading when you're nineteen instead of fourteen," he said. "It doesn't make any difference in the long run. But many of these kids think if you didn't read *Wuthering Heights* and *A Tale of Two Cities* when you were twelve, you're flawed for life. Some of them just despair and never get started, and some try to make a virtue of being ignorant as apes."

Whenever I am told anything of possible importance, I try to work it into a commentary. The following five points are addressed to young people.

1. You're probably reading this book by mistake. But keep reading.

2. It's not your fault that your level of awareness is akin to that of a tossed salad. You got a lousy deal. You were taught by the products of teachers' colleges. The culture has been corrupted by the TV industry, which is run by subhuman slime, and your parents are potheads.

3. I have it on good authority that if you start educating yourselves now, you still have a chance.

4. Good luck.

5. Stay away from me.

I Am Not a Schnook

Remember Jeb Stuart Magruder? He was a minor character in the Watergate scandal—came across as an oaf—did seven months in jail. Now he's a Presbyterian minister.

I read in the *Poughkeepsie Journal* that this Magruder guy— uh, Reverend Magruder—participated in a panel discussion on ethics.

He's quoted as saying, "In the first 200 years after the founding of this country, unethical behavior existed, but it was not tolerated. Today, I'm afraid unethical behavior is part of the norm . . . it is expected."

The article goes on: "Magruder cited an episode of 'The Oprah Winfrey Show' in which young women spoke about their lives as 'groupies,' fans who are obsessed with rock stars. One woman claimed to have had sex with about 2,000 musicians, he said.

"The woman appeared to be proud of her liaisons and 'obviously it was of interest to the public because it was on national television,' he said."

Now, I'm not claiming to be a normal person, or anything like that, but if I had been convicted of a crime against my nation—even after "paying my debt," as they say—I'd be embarrassed to go around volunteering my opinions on ethical questions. Even if I turned into a reverend—something which seems to happen quite a lot in prison—I think I'd stick to

theological topics. I'd leave pronouncements on ethics to min-
isters who had not gone away for a felony.

Besides, the example he gives—the groupie and the 2,000
rock musicians—isn't properly a question of ethics (unless maybe
she promised each of them that she'd be faithful).

What's more, the groupie did it with only 2,000 people—and
presumably they were aware it was being done. In my opinion
she's got Magruder beat in the areas of ethics, morals and good
taste—and she evidently gives better media than he does too.

That's why she was on "Oprah," Magruder—and you were
just an item of filler from the wire services. See, virtue is
rewarded.

Why I Don't Fly

I don't fly. Given that this is being written for a periodical especially addressed to matters atmospheric and above, I'd better expand on that statement. When I say I don't fly, I am not indicating that I do not personally operate an aircraft, as one might say, "I do not drive." When I say I do not fly, I mean as a passenger. I don't set foot on anything more apt to ascend than the escalator in Macy's.

A while back I wrote a piece about a boy's experience of model airplanes. A number of readers were kind enough to send letters commenting on the piece. Some liked it. One reader, a model-building enthusiast, was irate about my retrograde view that the old-fashioned "stick" models provided a more significant experience than the snap-together plastic toys now available in drugstores.

This reader complained that by my own admission I hadn't built a model since 1955, and therefore what right did I have to comment on the noble art of putting together model airplanes? He went on to ask whether this publication would run a piece on commercial air travel by someone who hadn't flown since that year.

Apparently. And, for all intents and purposes, this is it. In fact I was up in an airplane as recently as 1970. But I can imagine no reason compelling enough to cause me to go aloft

211

in the foreseeable future. This was not always the case. There was a time when I used to whiz about in the clouds like everybody else. In 1967 and 1968 airplanes took me around the world— something which used to be noteworthy, and the idea of which still gives me a thrill.

I've had a number of thrills aboard airplanes. I remember, with intense pleasure, crossing the Mediterranean on a night of breathtaking clarity, seeing a crescent moon with the horns pointing upward for the first time, and realizing that I was in the same sky the ancients had regarded.

Crossing the Alps on a brilliant summer day was noteworthy, and I certainly got a better idea of the Grand Canyon flying over it than standing on the edge.

I'm not against flying—I just tend not to do it. I have come to believe that opposing gravity is something not to be taken— uh, lightly.

If commercial space-shuttle flights should become a reality while I'm still in sound health, I'd hope to take one—but I'd plan on arriving at the launch site by train.

So why did I swear off air travel? those of you still reading may ask.

I'm not going to take any cheap shots, writing in this summer of 1987 wherein the nightly news regularly carries stories about near misses, pilot error, overbooking, and fifteen-hour delays. The commercial carriers are just going through an underregu- lated bad patch. A couple more major tragedies, and things will return to normal, I have no doubt.

It is true that knowing one is not going to fly allows one to confront the present situation with no need to rationalize—it's a fact, air travel is riskier than it was.

The risk I don't want to take, however, is that of having my memories of earlier flights obscured or corrupted. One of the virtues of being abstinent, or at least abstemious, in this regard is that I can clearly remember every flight I've ever been on. I like the antique idea of flying being not simply a convenience, but a singular alternative to be employed only when circumstances warrant. I quit flying when it became manifestly less romantic than bus travel.

I'm not one of those people who live in the past. I have a computer, a videocassette machine, a microwave oven. I don't decry progress and technology. I suppose I'd fly if I absolutely had to get somewhere in a big hurry—but what could be that important?

I'm certain I haven't given up anything I'd be likely to enjoy by staying off airliners. I've put friends on those mobile shopping malls that people travel in nowadays. They don't appeal to me. They relate to my recollections of air travel in about the same way taking an elevator ride would relate to climbing Kilimanjaro.

The canned music—the same boarding and debarking, wherever you are—the bored and irritated people, seats nowhere near a window, the ghastly routinization of it all—it's not for me. And the pathetic attempts to make it pleasant! The airlines advertise the comforts of the cabin as though it were a resort hotel—a ghastly resort hotel I'd never go to. They show films, for pity's sake! Something to pass the time, reduce the boredom, distract the passengers from the misery of being on an airplane. It was when they began to run box-office flops en route that I knew I was about to become a regular Amtrak customer.

It was different in the good old days. The first major airplane ride I ever took was a transatlantic crossing on a Boeing Constellation. It took something like fourteen hours, and it was in itself an adventure. There was romance in toiling across the ocean through the night. I recall my seat back was broken and I was forced to recline or sit pitched forward, hugging my knees, the whole way. It was a Sabena flight, and a strapping tall Belgian stewardess lurched up and down the aisle wielding pots of hot coffee. I had the feeling that during a moment of turbulence she would slosh a cupful of scalding java down the back of my neck—and sure enough, she did.

I was anything but out of sorts. Hemingway, writing about Africa, spoke of the discomforts one endures to make the experience real. It was like that. When I got off the plane, rumpled and stiff and scalded—I was in Europe. I knew I'd gotten somewhere.

Years later, traveling on local flights in Africa, I had some of the sweetest moments of my life. I remember waiting for the plane with a bunch of African friends. A little knot of people had gathered. They stood patiently gazing in the direction from which the plane would come. Not much more than an hour after its scheduled time, a tiny dot appeared over the mountains. People pointed, and spoke in hushed voices. They still knew a flying machine was miraculous, these Africans. There was none of the nervous and impatient chatter we hear in airports. The fact that people were arriving or departing, beginning or ending momentous journeys, was eclipsed by the magic and beauty of the machine, moving through the still air, the distant buzzing of its engines the only sound in the quiet afternoon.

When it landed, a good many minutes after having first been sighted, there were sighs, and expressions of wonder, amazement and love for the beautiful thing. You just don't get this at Newark International Airport.

It was my departing flight we had been waiting for. I shook hands solemnly with my African friends. They were aware of the magnitude of mystery and excitement inherent in sending one known to them away into the sky.

I took my place by a window on the side of the DC-3 with seats. The other side was full of cargo and livestock. There was no air conditioning, no pressurization, no piped music. There were enough holes in the airplane for plenty of fresh air to get in, and throughout the flight, we were never deprived of that particular fragrance readers who have traveled in East Africa will remember, and can never forget. I don't suppose we ever got much above a thousand feet. There was a perfect view of open grassland, and animals. I can distinctly picture giraffes running behind the shadow of the plane. In fact, I can't recall a single flight in Africa without giraffes at some point.

And there were giraffes to welcome us, as we landed in Nairobi toward dusk. These are the last hours of my last time in Africa I'm writing about. Every second is accounted for in my memory. I had a plate of curry and a bottle of beer alone in a dining room that bordered on a walled garden at Embakasi Airport. Going in and out of that airport for the previous two years, I'd never known there was a place of such charm there.

I ate my supper, and reflected on the events transacted in the time that was now coming to a close. I savored every remaining moment, every sound, every movement. I had the idea, and I still have it, that I was leaving a world where everything was pure reality, and returning to one that was an amalgam of the tame and the synthetic.

With the dust of the trail still on my boots, I boarded a Lufthansa airliner for Europe, where I would make my connection for home. Thank God, they didn't show a movie.

Play It Again, Wolfgang

It's said that a good deed doesn't count if you're found out. I've enjoyed this one for twenty-five years. I guess I can tell it now.

Richard and Louise were tiny people, thin, pale and quiet. They were utterly gentle little hipsters. They lived in New York, on Avenue C in the area known as alphabet city—a rough spot, where landlords would give you a reduction in rent if you'd get a large vicious dog, and people took turns going out of the apartment lest everything be stolen while they were away.

Louise was a painter of mystical, atmospheric pictures that took a year to complete, and Richard worked in a Zen restaurant on Seventh Street. They had a dog, but it was a sleepy old collie who liked everyone, and the junkies had gotten in and taken what valuables they had.

Richard and Louise were painfully poor, and forced to live in what amounted to a war zone, but they were neither embittered nor embattled. They were happy. They loved each other, and Art, and Philosophy, and vegetarian cooking. They were serious about cooking. They'd schlep bushel baskets of slightly bruised carrots and broccoli up to the apartment and make wonderful things with them.

I used to take my courage in my hands and go down to see them. The seven- or eight-block walk to the subway, late at night after visiting them, was as scary an experience as I care to remember.

Another friend of mine in those days was James Sacker, a radio broadcaster. He did the best classical music program ever, all night long, seven days a week. Jim was a Don Juan. He expended a lot of energy luring women up to his radio studio, which was in an office building in midtown, locked up like a fortress, after the cleaners had gone. Jim was one of those guys, of a type I don't seem to run into anymore, who admire people like Errol Flynn and John Barrymore, and regard seducing any and all women as the sacred obligation of all men. And naturally he assumed I was the same. To tell him any different would have certainly suggested to him that I was gay—and of course, he was phobic about gays. I let well enough alone. Mostly we talked about music.

On one occasion, Jim said to me, "Pinkwater, as you know, I never play requests—but for you, my friend, if there is ever a compelling reason—and there can be only one compelling reason for a real man—call me. I will play whatever selection you desire." The idea was that there would be some woman who would only go to bed with me if she heard Brandenburg Concerto Number Four.

I regarded the offer as having been made in the spirt of friendship. Jim was a sweet guy, in his weird way. And I enjoyed knowing I had the right to have a request played on his radio show.

So there I am, in alphabet city, having some cucumber soup with my little friends, and it's late at night, and they've got the radio on.

Louise says, "We miss *The Magic Flute* so much. We love it more than any other music. Ever since they took the records, we've been waiting for Sacker to play it—but he never does. Just *Don Giovanni*, all the time. It's been more than a year."

"I'm going to run downstairs and get a pack of cigarettes," I said.

Outside in the street, I found a pay phone, and made my call.

"Jim, it's Pinkwater. I can't talk long. Remember, you said you'd play a request?"

"I do," Jim said. "Is it a blonde or brunette?"

"She wants to hear *The Magic Flute*," I said.

By the time I had climbed the five flights back to the apartment, the overture had already begun.

"It's amazing," Richard whispered. "What a fantastic coincidence! Just after you left, he stopped the record he was playing—in the middle of the piece—and put on *The Magic Flute!*"

I sat on the sofa, and lit a cigarette. My friends and I listened to the opera, which ended just as dawn broke over the tenements.

Vintage Whines

Maybe it's just here in the Hudson Valley. Maybe it's everywhere. I first began to notice it when I moved here about eight years ago.

I'm talking about a particular attitude I run into when I have to transact business locally.

I might be in a store, for example—let's say a shoe store. I'll say, "Do you have a pair of Bebop Yupster basketball shoes, with imitation snakeskin trim in a size ten?" (My favorite sneaker—I will wear no other kind).

"Nope," says the clerk.

"What are those?" I ask, pointing.

"Those? Those are Bebop Yupster basketball shoes with imitation snakeskin trim," he says.

"Got a size ten?"

"Nope. All sold out."

"How about these?" I ask, pointing to a box marked size ten.

"What about 'em?"

"Mind if I try them on?"

"Suit yourself."

A while ago, we hired a young woman to clear some brush. She chopped down the seven-year-old lingonberry and gooseberry bushes—with berries on them—we'd shown her four times, and told her to be sure not to chop down. When this was pointed out to her, she screamed at my wife.

"You've got some nerve, putting me under pressure!" Then she took to whining. "I've got all these customers. It's so hard."

"It's your own business, right?" my wife asked.

"Yeh. So many customers. So much pressure. So hard."

I go into the supermarket. "I notice you're out of those imported Polish pickled pig's feet," I say to the manager. "Gonna get 'em in again soon?"

"Naw. The people keep buying them. Then we just have to restock the shelves."

"It's hard, isn't it?"

"Yeh."

Of course the girl who chopped the berry bushes will never work for us again—even if we were to ask her—after the way we mistreated her.

I found an ad. Lawns mowed. Brush cleared. No job too big, no job too small.

I called the number. "Want to do some mowing?"

"How big an area?"

"It's about an acre."

"No. That's too big."

"Your ad says no job too big, no job too small."

"Right—and that job's too big."

"I understand," I said. "No point knocking yourself out, right?"

"You got it, pal."

I suppose there's some conclusion to be drawn from all this—but I don't know. Writing these pieces is so hard.

Whiteouch

I called my mother in Los Angeles to find out how she fared in the earthquake. "Everything's fine," she said, "but I'm afraid to go to the bathroom." I didn't ask her what she thought the connection might be.

My mother believes that everything is somebody's fault. Hence, if anybody dies, somebody killed him. "It's that daughter of his. She killed him with those crazy hairdos."

So who was to blame for the disaster yesterday? It's the first week of October. Five inches or more of snow. The trees around here are in full leaf. They've just begun to get their fall colors. The heavy snow was sticking to the leaves and the trees were bending low.

Jill and I were outside when we heard the first crack—like a rifle shot. And the big willow split down the middle.

There's a hill behind the house with a stand of beautiful maples. They buckled and snapped in two. The trees all seemed to give way at once. We stood there weeping as one friend after another broke under the weight of the beautiful white stuff.

The power line got hit by a branch and killed the well pump and the electrically fired oil furnace.

"Maybe it's not so bad," I said. "Trees can take a lot."

"Shut up," Jill said. "Before you married me, you didn't know what a tree was."

Jill was following the tradition of her family, similar to mine.

I was contemplating the weeks of work, sawing and hauling—the sort of thing I hate. Preoccupied, I missed the moment. Jill seized it.

"This is your fault, you know."

According to ancient tradition, the first person to get blamed is stuck with it.

"My fault? Why's it my fault?"

"If you hadn't bored everybody last night talking about natural disasters and making jokes about your mother, this would never have happened."

Of course this exchange was making us feel much better. It would have been better still if I could have pinned it on Jill, but we were making headway. We were setting buckets under the eaves to collect water, digging for candles in kitchen drawers, locating the working flashlight, and putting together suitable survival clothing.

We spent an old-fashioned evening in the kitchen, heated by the gas stove and lit by candles. The phone lines had stayed up, and Jill chatted with her sister about how bad their mother treated them. It was cozy.

That was yesterday. It's bright and sunny today. The trees look pretty beat-up, but most of the maples will survive. So they're a little short—I love them anyway. It would cost a fortune to have someone come in and prune them like that.

Because It's There

Just above the the Hudson River is a small picnic area on
the grounds of the Vanderbilt Mansion National Historic
Site in Hyde Park, New York. This is where I'm getting ready
to ascend a steep incline to the level of the actual mansion—
some two hundred feet, over a distance of a half-mile.

I've been training all summer for this, and although I'm not
absolutely sure I'm ready, I don't think I can risk waiting any
longer. Fall showers and wet leaves tend to make for faulty
footing on the asphalt surface of the path—and there was that
freak snowstorm in early October last year.

I think I've got a pretty good chance today. I left all my
nonessential gear in the station wagon, when Jill dropped me
off. She's waiting for me in the visitors' parking lot at the top.
If she doesn't see me in two hours, she will begin a search—
but until that time, I'm on my own.

I've begun my ascent. The picnic area is below me now, and
I'm looking at the footbridge over the old New York Central
tracks. Last year there was an incident on the bridge involving
a party of Japanese tourists. One of them lost his lens cap, and
they had to descend down to the tracks to get it. There were no
serious injuries, but it could have been ugly.

I'm about a third of the way up the slope. It's heavy going. I've just come out of a wooded area where there were very bad mosquitoes. There's a really magnificent view of the rolling meadow below the mansion.

I think I'm about halfway now. I'm taking another rest. I met some natives of Hyde Park on the trail a little while ago. They're a cheerful people. They passed some remarks in the local dialect about how fat I am, and how I was sweating like a pig. Insolent swine . . . It's quite amazing how they scamper up and down these slopes in their boating shoes and plaid pants—but they're born to it.

OK. I'm nearly there. The air is a lot thinner up here. I'm in quite a bit of pain. One of my special mountaineering sneakers is chafing quite a lot, and I'm afraid I'm getting a blister. But I'm just going to press on.

This is it. I've just come all the way up to the level of the parking lot. I still have a half-mile to go, but it's flat all the way. I can even see the station wagon. Jill is waiting for me with an iced coffee and a biscuit from McDonald's. Life is good.

Well, it's over. That was this morning. Now, it's all receding into an exciting memory. I'm taking it easy—spread out on the couch. I've got tape on my blister. I feel at peace with myself and with nature. I faced the challenge of the Vanderbilt Mansion National Historic Site, and I think I gave a pretty good account of myself.

Would I do it again? Well, not right away.

Vox Populi

This is a story about radio broadcasting. When I moved up here to the country about nine years ago, I discovered this fantastic local radio station. It was a mom and pop operation— they'd built the station with their own hands—and it was just wonderful. They played a lot of classical music, good jazz, local news and talk—and they had two unique programs.

One was on every forenoon. The owner of the station would read aloud. He had a wonderful nonprofessional voice—the kind you seldom get to hear on radio (present company excepted), and he read whole books in installments. He read classics, current fiction, oddball favorites of his—he even read books of mine!

The other was "The Fred Show." "The Fred Show" was just splendid. It was a Saturday morning kid show. The real thing! This guy Fred is a ventriloquist, and he and his dummy, Harry, would host an authentic live radio program. It was humorous. Fred understands about humor for kids. What he understands is that the humor part is much more important than the "for kids" part. Fred knows every corny joke, song parody, and campfire routine that exists—and has a collection of all the comedy records that ever were. I never missed "The Fred Show."

So what happened? They moved Fred to Sundays at 9 P.M. I went to see the owner of the radio station. "Why'd you do that?"

"It isn't really a kids' show. Half his listeners are adults."

"Sure. I'm one of them. But the pleasure of it is that it's a *real* kids' show. How are the actual kids, the other half of his audience, going to hear him at 9 P.M. when they have to go to school the next day?"

"Well, he can make it a humor show. Our salesmen say he breaks up the day. It's easier to sell time when you have just one kind of thing all day long."

Country music is what they had now—they'd gotten rid of most of the classical music and jazz.

After a while Fred got fired.

The other good show—the one on which the owner used to read—had changed a lot. Now he spent most of the hour running quiz games. He'd found out that people like to call in to radio stations and win T-shirts for guessing riddles. He'd still read, but it's hard for the listener to stay with a novel in ten-minute snatches.

See, what this guy was doing—even though it was his very own radio station—was trying to please the greatest number of people. Instead of getting the listeners used to what he knew was good, he was making sure they got what they liked already. He was losing that which made his station unique and intrinsically valuable.

Pretty soon I quit listening—not enough to hold my interest. Lately, I heard that they'd sold the station to a local soft-pop AM station. It didn't matter to me one way or the other.

Today I got a call from a citizens' committee. They wanted me to come to a demonstration. They were protesting because the new owners had fired the former owner from his reading-aloud show, which was supposed to continue under the new management. I guess they think he breaks up the day.

"What's the matter with you?" I asked the protesters. "Don't you like Tennessee Ernie and Liberace?" I told them I wouldn't protest. I believe in a free market, just like Ronald Reagan. I believe that left alone, things will find their own level.

Just the Fundamentals

I'd like to say a word in favor of fundamentalists. They're getting a bad rap.

The dictionary says that fundamentalism is a movement in twentieth-century Protestantism emphasizing as fundamental the literal inerrancy of the Scriptures, the second coming of Jesus Christ, the virgin birth, and so on. Also a movement or attitude similar to Protestant Fundamentalism.

I don't happen to subscribe to any of those beliefs, but it's a point of view, and some of the people I've encountered whose point of view it is are very nice people.

The bad rap comes from a confusion of fundamentalism and fanaticism. "Moslem fundamentalists [meaning terrorists] did thus and so," the media will report. Most all, if not all, Moslems are fundamentalists—that doesn't mean they all want to blow people up.

I hear from fundamentalists—kids and adults—in my role as an author of children's books. I hear from bigots and fanatics too—but they're not automatically the same people.

Here's a case that comes up from time to time: I'll get a letter from a kid, or a class, commending me for not using profanity in books I write. Sometimes, there's an explicit religious connection made, sometimes not. Sometimes the letter comes from a religious school.

I write back to the kid or the class, and explain that I do not, as a rule, use vulgar language in books I write for kids as a matter of choice and preference—but that I would not hesitate to use it if the story called for it. For example, if I wrote a character who cussed—I'd have him cuss. It wouldn't bother me.

I go on to explain that it's a good idea to be able to distinguish between polite and impolite language, and to try to respect people's sensibilities—but that I do not believe that words have power within themselves, and by making a special case of certain words and expressions, we imbue them with a power they should not have.

I tell them that I use vulgar language around the house, and when I'm alone, I use nothing else.

Then I suggest—now get this—that maybe they'd like to show my letter to their teacher, pastor or parents, and maybe have a discussion with them, or their class, and compare their ideas on the subject with mine.

And they do it! What do you think of that? These fundamentalist kids, or their teacher, will write back to me and say that they had an interesting talk based on my letter. I don't expect anyone changes their basic views—but they're willing to take a look at mine.

They're not so bad.

Of course, I'm not talking about the educator from down south who accused me of being a satanist because I wrote a story about a werewolf—but that guy would be a pain in the posterior whatever he believed.

Talis

My father liked a synagogue on the south side. It was a wooden building that hadn't seen a coat of paint in a hundred years. I never heard it referred to as anything but the *Varshava Shul*, the Warsaw Synagogue. It was your basic, Orthodox, bare-knuckles shul. All the congregants were from Poland, and most of them appeared to be ex-gangsters like my father. Guys with broken noses and gold teeth.

There were 360 opinions about the proper direction to face during prayer—and the Jews vied to be the first to finish reading a passage, after which they would slam the book shut and look around defiantly. Not one of them could understand Hebrew—just read it fast.

On the way home from services, my father might stop off in the neighborhood and buy a pound of sliced baked Virgina ham. He saw no inconsistency in this.

"Spare ribs would be different," my father would say. "There's no disrespect in ham as good as this."

That's how my father practiced his religion. I have no reason to believe God was ever dissatisfied with him.

Once I accompanied my father to Los Angeles. A grandson was about to undergo the bar-mitzvah ordeal.

The event was to take place in a fancy synagogue. It looked like one of those old-fashioned deluxe movie houses. I think the building and grounds were supposed to be a Hollywood-style replica of the City of Jerusalem in Roman times. Only bigger.

Bigger even than the synagogue was the reputation of the rabbi they had there. He had studied with the greatest voice and elocution coaches in Hollywood. He sounded the way God would sound—if He'd had the lessons.

When we arrived in L.A., it turned out that this mega-rabbi wanted my father to come and see him in his study.

"Rabbi Mishkin, who talks like Charlton Heston, wants to see *me*?" my father asked.

"Right away," my sister said. She seemed nervous. Something was up.

I recognized Rabbi Mishkin's office immediately. It had been used to shoot the throne-room scenes in the movie *The Black Shield of Falworth*.

The rabbi entered. "Mr. Pinkwater. You're a simple man, a peasant from Europe. I'll speak to you in words you'll understand. You represent the backwardness, ignorance and superstition of the Middle Ages."

This must have rankled my father. He was a fierce modernist. He resented the nineteenth century, let alone the Middle Ages.

"Get to the point," he said to Rabbi Mishkin.

"The point is," Rabbi Mishkin said, "you will *not* put on a prayer shawl in this temple."

"I will not?"

"You absolutely will not. I forbid it."

Rabbi Mishkin knew how to talk to these old Jews. He knew that they wouldn't disobey a direct order from a rabbi.

The prayer shawl, or talis: in the Book of Numbers, God tells Moses to have the children of Israel put fringes at the corners of their garments, and a thread of blue. In regarding this, they are to remember the sea and the sky and the creations of God, and His commandments.

"I will not put on a prayer shawl at the bar mitzvah of my grandson?" my father asked.

"Naturally, you're confused," Mishkin said. "I'll explain as simply as I can. This is a modern house of worship. We break with the practices of the past, quaint and colorful as they may be. Many of our members bring their Christian friends to services here. We don't want them to see old men with beards bobbing around, acting crazy. We don't want them to see anything foreign and strange. We want them to see . . ."

"That we're just the same as them!" my father said.

"Yes! Exactly!" the rabbi beamed.

"Thank you, rabbi," my father stood up. We left his office.

We went to a religious goods shop and bought the two biggest, richest-looking talisim they had, made of lamb's wool with thick black stripes. We went early to the synagogue to make sure we had seats in the front, and the center.

When we say we subscribe to the faith of our fathers, we usually mean the father we knew. Also, there's a tendency for each generation to liberalize the belief. As the son of a ham-eating, iconoclastic, free-style Jew, I was well on the way to becoming no Jew at all. What I was about to do was defy the obnoxious rabbi, and support my father in a sentimental gesture. The talis had no particular meaning for me.

And yet, when we gathered the fringes to our lips, kissing them as an expression of respect and love for God's commandments—when we stood and spread the ancient garments on our arms, like birds drying their wings, for a moment, before enveloping ourselves in whiteness—it came to me, strongly, that this precise activity had been carried on, by people . . . by my forebears, for thousands of years.